Jay Payleitner

Graphics by Rex Bohn

HARVEST HOUSE PUBLISHERS
EUGENE, OREGON

Cover by Dual Identity, Inc.

The Dad Manifesto poster by Rex Bohn

Published in association with the Steve Laube Agency, LLC, 5025 N. Central Ave., #635, Phoenix, Arizona 85012.

THE DAD MANIFESTO
Copyright © 2016 Jay Payleitner
Published by Harvest House Publishers
Eugene, Oregon 97402
www.harvesthousepublishers.com

ISBN 978-0-7369-6360-2 (pbk.)
ISBN 978-0-7369-6361-9 (eBook)

Printed in China

16 17 18 19 20 21 22 23 24 / RDS-JC / 10 9 8 7 6 5 4 3 2 1

To my kids.
And yours.

STOP AND CATCH THE FIREFLIES. LAUGH WITH THEM. CRY WITH THEM. GIVE NOOGIES.

ANSWER THEIR QUESTIONS WITH QUESTIONS.

DON'T CURSE THE TRAIN, COUNT THE CARS.

SPY ON YOUR KIDS. BUY A UNICYCLE.

SNUGGLE. RESPECT THEIR MOM.

LAUGH OVER SPILT MILK. QUIT SMOKING.

RESPOND TO ANY CRISIS, "I LOVE YOU. IT'LL BE OKAY. WE'LL GET THROUGH THIS TOGETHER."

HOLD YOUR BABY. TUCK IN. SAY BEDTIME PRAYERS.

RAKE LEAVES TOGETHER. STOP RAKING TO WATCH THE GEESE FLY SOUTH IN 'V' FORMATION.

IGNORE THE STICKBALL DENTS ON THE GARAGE DOOR.

WAKE YOUR KID FOR A LUNAR ECLIPSE. MAKE STILTS.

QUIT GOLF. OR PATIENTLY TEACH THEM TO PLAY GOLF. SUDDENLY YOUR 8-YEAR-OLD IS LOOKING YOU IN THE EYE.

TEACH ROCK/PAPER/SCISSORS. TELL KNOCK-KNOCK JOKES. GIVE HORSEY RIDES.

PLAY H-O-R-S-E.

DON'T LET THEM WIN. THEY'LL BEAT YOU FAIR AND SQUARE SOON ENOUGH.

EARN THE RIGHT TO SAY WHAT NEEDS TO BE SAID.

CHAT OVER WAFFLES.

STOP AT HISTORICAL MARKERS.

SKIP ROCKS.

The **DAD** MANIFESTO

52 THINGS FOR FOREVER FATHERS TO NEVER FORGET

KISS YOUR WIFE IN THE KITCHEN.

DON'T BE THE JERK IN THE STANDS.

CHAPERONE A SCHOOL DANCE.

CUDDLE.

ALWAYS HAVE A CLEAN HANDKERCHIEF.

VOLUNTEER AT THEIR SCHOOL OR YOUTH GROUP.

WRITE "LOVE YOU" ON A STICKY NOTE. APOLOGIZE

KEEP PROMISES. SOMETIMES SAY NO. WHEN YOU MESS UP.

RESCUE THEM AT THE TOP OF ANY SLIPPERY SLOPE.

MAKE TIME FOR THEM. THEY'LL MAKE TIME FOR YOU LATER. CARRY RECENT PHOTOS ON YOUR SMARTPHONE.

BE AMAZED WHEN THEY BRING YOU A BUG, DANDELION, OR SHINY ROCK.

MAKE YOUR HOME A HANGOUT.

CALL, TEXT, OR REACH OUT TO THEM RIGHT NOW.

BE THERE, DAD. BE AN AWESOME GRANDPA.

TEACH THEM HOW TO LOVE.

TEACH THEM HOW TO BE LOVED.

The Dad Manifesto © 2014
Words By Jay Payleitner,
Author/Speaker, jaypayleitner.com
Design by Rex Bohn, rexbohn.com

The DAD MANIFESTO
A Brief History

At conferences, I—like many authors and speakers— spend a fair amount of time sitting or standing at a book table chatting with attendees, signing books, and making new friends.

We'll stack a dozen titles on the table, and hopefully the different topics and book covers generate a little buzz and a little traffic.

But the item on the book table that usually gets the *most* attention is not a book at all. In the corner of the table, we'll typically prop up a 12-inch by 18-inch framed version of *The Dad Manifesto*. It often draws a small crowd.

Men especially nudge each other and point to an item on the framed poster and say, "I do that," or "That's a great idea," or "I wish I knew this stuff 20 years ago." When a dad takes home a copy, I imagine that piece of artwork hanging in his office, den, or workshop.

I originally conceived *The Dad Manifesto* as a series of thought-provoking ideas to remind fathers of ways to connect with our kids. To love, engage, and share life with those smaller humans we love so much.

It was just a list.

Some of the ideas are meant to be taken literally. Some are metaphors or symbolic examples of a larger truth. Actually, most of the ideas are both. For example, I believe dads *should* buy a unicycle for their ten-year-old. But the bigger idea is that dads should constantly be looking for opportunities to open doors for their kids.

Other examples: "Give Noogies" and "Hold Your Baby" are really about making physical contact with our kids. "Skip Rocks" is about rekindling fond memories from our own childhood—especially stuff we may have learned from our dads. "Make Stilts" is about seeing our children as future adults.

As a radio producer and scriptwriter, I have long placed high value on writing short pieces—using as *few* words as possible to say as *much* as possible. During talks, I typically throw short phrases on a screen, tell a humorous or heartfelt story, and spell out the underlying principle. Many of the "rules" in *The Dad Manifesto* have previously appeared as chapter titles in my books.

The early typed and printed list of "52 Things for Forever Fathers to Never Forget" actually looked pretty boring from a design perspective. Not to mention the list seemed long, laborious, and burdensome.

That's when I brought the list to my friend, Rex Bohn, an inspired designer and illustrator. Rex had done illustrations for three of my earlier books, and he instantly saw the potential of the project.

Rex chose the type fonts, created the visually appealing flow, and sprinkled in a few tasteful and inspired illustrations. That's when *The Dad Manifesto* took on a life of its own. Printed in a standard letter size, it became a conference handout. Digitally printed on white linen stock, it became a piece of art suitable for framing. Slingshot Publishing discovered the concept and developed an even larger poster, a wall plaque, and a traveling coffee mug.

This book is the most recent rendition. It fleshes out the background of the 52 ideas in the manifesto and reveals how each item completes a different piece of the fathering puzzle.

Will *The Dad Manifesto* sweep across the nation and help create a generation of fathers who give noogies, make stilts, skip rocks, quit smoking, and pull over to catch fireflies? That's probably too much to expect.

Really, the only impact we can have is on our own children. And our children's children. And maybe our friends, neighbors, and coworkers. And their children. And maybe...

Well, first things first.

Seek first his kingdom and his righteousness,
and all these things will be given to you as well.
MATTHEW 6:33

STOP AND CATCH THE FIREFLIES.

*For where your treasure is, there
your heart will be also.*

MATTHEW 6:21

A friend told me his favorite memory growing up. He was eight or nine and vividly remembers driving with his dad on a two-lane country road at twilight. His father went on lots of business trips and always wore wingtips and a three-piece suit. Suddenly, this dad pulls off onto the shoulder and jumps out of the car. For a moment, it was scary for my friend. The dad grabs a glass jar out of the trunk and motions his son to follow him out into the grassy field...to catch lightning bugs. Ten minutes later, the car is back on the road carrying muddy wingtips, a jar of fireflies, and a wonderstruck little boy.

The number one rule of *The Dad Manifesto*: To make memories, stop and catch the fireflies.

STOP AND CATCH THE FIREFLIES. **LAUGH WITH THEM. CRY WITH THEM.** GIVE NOOGIES. ANSWER THEIR QUESTIONS WITH QUESTIONS. DON'T CURSE THE TRAIN, COUNT THE CARS. SPY ON YOUR KIDS. BUY A UNICYCLE. SNUGGLE. RESPECT THEIR MOM. LAUGH OVER SPILT MILK. QUIT SMOKING. RESPOND TO ANY CRISIS, "I LOVE YOU. IT'LL BE OKAY. WE'LL GET THROUGH THIS TOGETHER." HOLD YOUR BABY. TUCK IN. SAY BEDTIME PRAYERS. RAKE LEAVES TOGETHER. STOP RAKING TO WATCH THE GEESE FLY SOUTH IN "V" FORMATION. IGNORE THE STICKBALL DENTS ON THE GARAGE DOOR. WAKE YOUR KID FOR A LUNAR ECLIPSE. MAKE STILTS. SUDDENLY YOUR 8-YEAR-OLD IS LOOKING YOU IN THE EYE. QUIT GOLF. OR PATIENTLY TEACH THEM TO PLAY GOLF. TEACH ROCK/PAPER/SCISSORS. TELL KNOCK-KNOCK JOKES. GIVE HORSEY RIDES. PLAY H-O-R-S-E. DON'T LET THEM WIN. THEY'LL BEAT YOU FAIR AND SQUARE SOON ENOUGH.

The DAD MANIFESTO 52 THINGS FOR FOREVER FATHERS TO NEVER FORGET

KISS YOUR WIFE IN THE KITCHEN. DON'T BE THE JERK IN THE STANDS. CHAPERONE A SCHOOL DANCE. EARN THE RIGHT TO SAY WHAT NEEDS TO BE SAID. CHAT OVER WAFFLES. STOP AT HISTORICAL MARKERS. CUDDLE. SKIP ROCKS. ALWAYS HAVE A CLEAN HANDKERCHIEF. VOLUNTEER AT THEIR SCHOOL OR YOUTH GROUP. WRITE "LOVE YOU" ON A STICKY NOTE. APOLOGIZE KEEP PROMISES. SOMETIMES SAY NO. WHEN YOU MESS UP. RESCUE THEM AT THE TOP OF ANY SLIPPERY SLOPE. MAKE TIME FOR THEM. THEY'LL MAKE TIME FOR YOU LATER. CARRY RECENT PHOTOS ON YOUR SMARTPHONE. BE AMAZED WHEN THEY BRING YOU A BUG, DANDELION, OR SHINY ROCK. MAKE YOUR HOME A HANGOUT. CALL, TEXT, OR REACH OUT TO THEM RIGHT NOW. BE THERE, DAD. BE AN AWESOME GRANDPA. TEACH THEM HOW TO LOVE. TEACH THEM HOW TO BE LOVED.

The Dad Manifesto © 2012
Words by Jay Payleitner.
AuthorSpeaker. jaypayleitner.com
Design by Ken Bonn. textedin.com

LAUGH WITH THEM.
CRY WITH THEM.

Rejoice with those who rejoice, and
weep with those who weep.

ROMANS 12:15 NASB

When our kids come to us with emotional news, why do dads often respond with the opposite emotion?

Your third-grader proudly shows you their pinewood derby car and you point out some minor fault. Your daughter gets dumped by her boyfriend and you say, "He was a jerk anyway." Your son is excited about his new spot on the JV team, but you ask how soon he will make varsity. Your high school senior shows you an acceptance letter to one college, but you shrug it off and ask if they've heard from a more prestigious school. Not cool, Dad.

Instead, come alongside them. Cheer their good news and mourn their disappointments. Later you can guide, offer other options, or push them to the next level of achievement. But don't throw cold water on their successes. And don't minimize their grief.

STOP AND CATCH THE FIREFLIES. LAUGH WITH THEM. CRY WITH THEM. **GIVE NOOGIES.**

ANSWER THEIR QUESTIONS WITH QUESTIONS. DON'T CURSE THE TRAIN, COUNT THE CARS.

SPY ON YOUR KIDS. BUY A UNICYCLE.

SNUGGLE. RESPECT THEIR MOM.

LAUGH OVER SPILT MILK. **QUIT SMOKING.**

RESPOND TO ANY CRISIS, "I LOVE YOU. IT'LL BE OKAY. WE'LL GET THROUGH THIS TOGETHER."

HOLD YOUR BABY. TUCK IN. SAY BEDTIME PRAYERS. RAKE LEAVES TOGETHER. STOP RAKING TO WATCH THE GEESE FLY SOUTH IN "V" FORMATION.

IGNORE THE STICKBALL DENTS ON THE GARAGE DOOR.

WAKE YOUR KID FOR A LUNAR ECLIPSE. MAKE STILTS. SUDDENLY YOUR 8-YEAR-OLD IS LOOKING YOU IN THE EYE.

QUIT GOLF. OR PATIENTLY TEACH THEM TO PLAY GOLF.

TEACH ROCK/PAPER/SCISSORS. TELL KNOCK-KNOCK JOKES. GIVE HORSEY RIDES.

PLAY H-O-R-S-E. DON'T LET THEM WIN. THEY'LL BEAT YOU FAIR AND SQUARE SOON ENOUGH.

KISS YOUR WIFE IN THE KITCHEN. DON'T BE THE JERK IN THE STANDS. **CHAPERONE** A SCHOOL DANCE.

The **DAD** MANIFESTO 52 THINGS FOR FOREVER FATHERS TO NEVER FORGET

EARN THE RIGHT TO SAY WHAT NEEDS TO BE SAID. **CUDDLE.**

CHAT OVER WAFFLES. STOP AT HISTORICAL MARKERS.

SKIP ROCKS. ALWAYS HAVE A CLEAN HANDKERCHIEF.

VOLUNTEER AT THEIR SCHOOL OR YOUTH GROUP.

WRITE "LOVE YOU" ON A STICKY NOTE. **APOLOGIZE** KEEP PROMISES. SOMETIMES SAY NO. WHEN YOU MESS UP.

RESCUE THEM AT THE TOP OF ANY SLIPPERY SLOPE.

MAKE TIME FOR THEM. **CARRY RECENT PHOTOS** THEY'LL MAKE TIME FOR YOU LATER. **ON YOUR SMARTPHONE.**

BE AMAZED MAKE YOUR HOME A HANGOUT. WHEN THEY BRING YOU A BUG, DANDELION, OR SHINY ROCK. CALL, TEXT, OR REACH OUT TO THEM RIGHT NOW.

BE THERE, DAD. BE AN AWESOME GRANDPA.

TEACH THEM HOW TO LOVE. **TEACH THEM HOW TO BE LOVED.**

The Dad Manifesto © 2014

GIVE NOOGIES.

*God decided in advance to adopt us into
his own family by bringing us to himself
through Jesus Christ. This is what he wanted
to do, and it gave him great pleasure.*

EPHESIANS 1:5 NLT

The joy of fatherhood should overflow into making physical connections with sons and daughters at every age and stage.

When they're babies, burble their tummies and squeeze their toes. Toddlers need to be rassled and tumbled. During grade school, it's hugs, tickles, and noogies. That leads right into other physical contact as they mature, including dancing with your daughter and instructions on how to give a good, firm, respectful handshake. For the record, all kids—if they choose—should be able to sit in their dad's lap anytime.

When it comes to noogies, bear hugs, tickling, and wrestling, we're not talking about abuse. As a matter of fact, *healthy* physical contact between dads and kids helps build protection against all kinds of *unhealthy* contact.

STOP AND CATCH THE FIREFLIES. LAUGH WITH THEM. CRY WITH THEM. GIVE NOOGIES.

ANSWER THEIR QUESTIONS WITH QUESTIONS.

DON'T CURSE THE TRAIN, COUNT THE CARS.

SPY ON YOUR KIDS. BUY A UNICYCLE.

SNUGGLE. RESPECT THEIR MOM.

LAUGH OVER SPILT MILK. QUIT SMOKING.

RESPOND TO ANY CRISIS, "I LOVE YOU. IT'LL BE OKAY. WE'LL GET THROUGH THIS TOGETHER."

HOLD YOUR BABY. TUCK IN. SAY BEDTIME PRAYERS.

RAKE LEAVES TOGETHER.

STOP RAKING TO WATCH THE GEESE FLY SOUTH IN "V" FORMATION.

IGNORE THE STICKBALL DENTS ON THE GARAGE DOOR. MAKE STILTS.

WAKE YOUR KID FOR A LUNAR ECLIPSE. SUDDENLY YOUR 8-YEAR-OLD IS LOOKING YOU IN THE EYE.

QUIT GOLF. OR PATIENTLY TEACH THEM TO PLAY GOLF.

TEACH ROCK/PAPER/SCISSORS. TELL KNOCK-KNOCK JOKES. GIVE HORSEY RIDES.

PLAY H-O-R-S-E. DON'T LET THEM WIN. THEY'LL BEAT YOU FAIR AND SQUARE SOON ENOUGH.

The DAD MANIFESTO
52 THINGS FOR FOREVER FATHERS TO NEVER FORGET

KISS YOUR WIFE IN THE KITCHEN. DON'T BE THE JERK IN THE STANDS.

CHAPERONE A SCHOOL DANCE.

EARN THE RIGHT TO SAY WHAT NEEDS TO BE SAID.

CHAT OVER WAFFLES. CUDDLE.

STOP AT HISTORICAL MARKERS.

SKIP ROCKS. ALWAYS HAVE A CLEAN HANDKERCHIEF.

VOLUNTEER AT THEIR SCHOOL OR YOUTH GROUP.

WRITE "LOVE YOU" ON A STICKY NOTE. APOLOGIZE

KEEP PROMISES. SOMETIMES SAY NO. WHEN YOU MESS UP.

RESCUE THEM AT THE TOP OF ANY SLIPPERY SLOPE.

MAKE TIME FOR THEM. CARRY RECENT PHOTOS
THEY'LL MAKE TIME FOR YOU LATER. ON YOUR SMARTPHONE.

BE AMAZED MAKE YOUR HOME A HANGOUT.

CALL, TEXT, OR REACH OUT TO THEM RIGHT NOW.

WHEN THEY BRING YOU A BUG, DANDELION, OR SHINY ROCK.

BE THERE, DAD. BE AN AWESOME GRANDPA.

TEACH THEM HOW TO LOVE.

TEACH THEM HOW TO BE LOVED.

The Dad Manifesto ® 2014
Words By Jay Payleitner
Author/Speaker, JayPayleitner.com
Design by Rex Bohn, rexbohn.com

4

ANSWER
THEIR QUESTIONS
WITH QUESTIONS.

*"What is written in the Law?" [Jesus]
replied. "How do you read it?"*

LUKE 10:26

When asked about whether it is right to pay taxes to Caesar, Jesus asked, "Whose image is on the Roman coin?" When an expert in the law asked, "Who is my neighbor?" Jesus told the parable of the good Samaritan and then asked which of the three men was a neighbor to the man in need of help.

Dads can use the same strategy. When a kid asks, "How come there are no stars tonight?" don't just say, "It's cloudy." That ends the conversation. Instead, ask followup questions: "Where do you think they are?" "Are the stars still there?" "What could be hiding the stars?" Then expand their minds. "What are stars anyway?" "What's the closest star?" "Who put those stars there?"

Answering their questions with questions gets them thinking. And that's a good thing.

STOP AND CATCH THE FIREFLIES. LAUGH WITH THEM. CRY WITH THEM. GIVE NOOGIES.

ANSWER THEIR QUESTIONS WITH QUESTIONS.

DON'T CURSE THE TRAIN, COUNT THE CARS.

SPY ON YOUR KIDS. BUY A UNICYCLE.

SNUGGLE. RESPECT THEIR MOM.

LAUGH OVER SPILT MILK. QUIT SMOKING.

RESPOND TO ANY CRISIS, "I LOVE YOU. IT'LL BE OKAY. WE'LL GET THROUGH THIS TOGETHER."

HOLD YOUR BABY. TUCK IN. SAY BEDTIME PRAYERS.

RAKE LEAVES TOGETHER. STOP RAKING TO WATCH THE GEESE FLY SOUTH IN "V" FORMATION.

IGNORE THE STICKBALL DENTS ON THE GARAGE DOOR.

WAKE YOUR KID FOR A LUNAR ECLIPSE. MAKE STILTS. SUDDENLY YOUR 8-YEAR-OLD IS LOOKING YOU IN THE EYE.

QUIT GOLF. OR PATIENTLY TEACH THEM TO PLAY GOLF.

TEACH ROCK/PAPER/SCISSORS. TELL KNOCK-KNOCK JOKES. GIVE HORSEY RIDES.

PLAY H-O-R-S-E. DON'T LET THEM WIN. THEY'LL BEAT YOU FAIR AND SQUARE SOON ENOUGH.

The DAD MANIFESTO 52 THINGS FOR FOREVER FATHERS TO NEVER FORGET

KISS YOUR WIFE IN THE KITCHEN. DON'T BE THE JERK IN THE STANDS. CHAPERONE A SCHOOL DANCE.

EARN THE RIGHT TO SAY WHAT NEEDS TO BE SAID.

CHAT OVER WAFFLES.

STOP AT HISTORICAL MARKERS. CUDDLE.

SKIP ROCKS. ALWAYS HAVE A CLEAN HANDKERCHIEF.

VOLUNTEER AT THEIR SCHOOL OR YOUTH GROUP.

WRITE "LOVE YOU" ON A STICKY NOTE. APOLOGIZE

KEEP PROMISES. SOMETIMES SAY NO. WHEN YOU MESS UP.

RESCUE THEM AT THE TOP OF ANY SLIPPERY SLOPE.

MAKE TIME FOR THEM. THEY'LL MAKE TIME FOR YOU LATER. CARRY RECENT PHOTOS ON YOUR SMARTPHONE.

BE AMAZED WHEN THEY BRING YOU A BUG, DANDELION, OR SHINY ROCK.

MAKE YOUR HOME A HANGOUT. CALL, TEXT, OR REACH OUT TO THEM RIGHT NOW.

BE THERE, DAD. BE AN AWESOME GRANDPA.

TEACH THEM HOW TO LOVE.

TEACH THEM HOW TO BE LOVED.

The Dad Manifesto © 2014 Based on Jay Payleitner's book/speaker, jaypayleitner.com Design by Ken Dewey, kenaude.com

DON'T CURSE THE TRAIN, COUNT THE CARS.

Dear brothers and sisters, when troubles of any kind come your way, consider it an opportunity for great joy. For you know that when your faith is tested, your endurance has a chance to grow. So let it grow, for when your endurance is fully developed, you will be perfect and complete, needing nothing.

JAMES 1:2-4 NLT

Yes, freight trains are frustrating. But while you're muttering under your breath, your eight-year-old in the backseat is gleefully counting the cars!

Here's an idea, Dad. Model patience. Especially in those critical years when your son or daughter is watching your every move, look at any trouble or inconvenience as a way to demonstrate that you trust God. Maybe even look for teachable moments.

Let those train cars zipping past trigger a dialogue. Topics might include what that train might be carrying, where it might be headed, why railroad tracks must be parallel, or why going around railroad gates is an extremely bad idea. Or you could simply... count the cars.

SPY ON YOUR KIDS.

*I urge you, brothers and sisters, to watch out
for those who cause divisions and put obstacles
in your way that are contrary to the teaching
you have learned. Keep away from them.*

ROMANS 16:17

You need to know stuff about your kids that they don't know you know.

Network with other parents. Be tech savvy. Get to know their friends. Don't sneak into your teenager's room and read their diary. But absolutely be aware of the books they read, music they listen to, and videos they watch. Your goal is not to bust them for minor bad decisions. Your goal is to know who they are and how they see themselves so you can help them chase their dreams and reach their potential.

They trust you to not be a snoop. But they also trust you to do whatever it takes to protect them from evil. Which means if you have hard evidence your child is making choices that threaten their well-being, you need to respond. Whatever it takes.

BUY A UNICYCLE.

Test all things; hold fast what is good.
1 THESSALONIANS 5:21 NKJV

There's a unicycle hanging in my garage. It's never been ridden. And that's okay.

We bought it for Randy's ninth birthday. He tried it. His brothers and sister tried it. Neighbors and friends tried it. No one chose to put in the time to master the one-wheeled beast. Again, that's okay. Our job as dads is to open doors.

Such as? Art. Athletics. Music. Astronomy. Stand-up comedy. Poetry. Chess. Photography. Computer programming. Culinary arts. Spelunking. Pyrotechnics. Juggling. Dance. Filmmaking. If you see a spark of interest, open the door and let your kids try a new skill under your watchful guidance. Maybe right in your driveway. They may try it and say, "No thanks." *Or* they may master a new skill and run off and join the circus. Which, again, is really okay. Right?

SNUGGLE.

"For I know the plans I have for you," declares the LORD, "plans to prosper you and not to harm you, plans to give you hope and a future."

JEREMIAH 29:11

Snuggling and cuddling are both part of *The Dad Manifesto*. Despite what the dictionary might say, they are quite different. While cuddling is an end goal, snuggling is a gateway to other activities.

Snuggling with our kids describes intimate moments of discovery, whispering, plotting, and dreaming. On a couch watching old movies. In a cozy corner reading a picture book. On a log watching a dancing campfire. At bedtime with moonbeams streaming in the window.

During a good snuggle, you and your child—of any age—are establishing a pattern of trust and communication. Snuggling is when make-believe morphs into reality. That's when your child will first start to think, *Maybe I can be anything, maybe God has a special plan for me, maybe I can make a difference in this world.*

9

RESPECT THEIR MOM.

A wife of noble character who can find? She is worth far more than rubies. Her husband has full confidence in her and lacks nothing of value. She brings him good, not harm, all the days of her life.

PROVERBS 31:10-12

I have a fantastic wife. If it weren't for Rita, I would be living in a van down by the river. She's easy to love and has earned my respect and admiration.

Honestly, I don't know what it's like to be in long-term conflict with my wife, separated or divorced, scraping up child support, and agonizing because I can't see my kids. If that describes your life, then my heart aches for you and your entire family.

Dad, if you've been through a divorce, you may have some extra work to do. Accept responsibility for past mistakes. Treat your children's mom with dignity. Refrain from shouting, blaming, or name-calling. Respond to her requests and make accommodations with fairness and respect.

Grace, common courtesy, and communication are minimum requirements for all family relationships.

STOP AND CATCH THE FIREFLIES. LAUGH WITH THEM. CRY WITH THEM. GIVE NOOGIES.

ANSWER THEIR QUESTIONS WITH QUESTIONS.

DON'T CURSE THE TRAIN, COUNT THE CARS.

SPY ON YOUR KIDS. BUY A UNICYCLE.

SNUGGLE. RESPECT THEIR MOM.

LAUGH OVER SPILT MILK. QUIT SMOKING.

RESPOND TO ANY CRISIS, "I LOVE YOU. IT'LL BE OKAY. WE'LL GET THROUGH THIS TOGETHER."

HOLD YOUR BABY. TUCK IN. SAY BEDTIME PRAYERS.

RAKE LEAVES TOGETHER.

STOP RAKING TO WATCH THE GEESE FLY SOUTH IN "V" FORMATION.

IGNORE THE STICKBALL DENTS ON THE GARAGE DOOR.

WAKE YOUR KID FOR A LUNAR ECLIPSE. MAKE STILTS. SUDDENLY YOUR 8-YEAR-OLD IS LOOKING YOU IN THE EYE.

QUIT GOLF. OR PATIENTLY TEACH THEM TO PLAY GOLF.

TEACH ROCK/PAPER/SCISSORS. TELL KNOCK-KNOCK JOKES. GIVE HORSEY RIDES.

PLAY H-O-R-S-E. KISS YOUR WIFE IN THE KITCHEN.

DON'T LET THEM WIN. THEY'LL BEAT YOU FAIR AND SQUARE SOON ENOUGH.

DON'T BE THE JERK IN THE STANDS.

CHAPERONE A SCHOOL DANCE.

EARN THE RIGHT TO SAY WHAT NEEDS TO BE SAID.

CHAT OVER WAFFLES.

STOP AT HISTORICAL MARKERS. CUDDLE.

SKIP ROCKS. ALWAYS HAVE A CLEAN HANDKERCHIEF.

VOLUNTEER AT THEIR SCHOOL OR YOUTH GROUP.

WRITE "LOVE YOU" ON A STICKY NOTE. APOLOGIZE

KEEP PROMISES. SOMETIMES SAY NO. WHEN YOU MESS UP.

RESCUE THEM AT THE TOP OF ANY SLIPPERY SLOPE.

MAKE TIME FOR THEM. THEY'LL MAKE TIME FOR YOU LATER. CARRY RECENT PHOTOS ON YOUR SMARTPHONE.

BE AMAZED WHEN THEY BRING YOU A BUG, DANDELION, OR SHINY ROCK. MAKE YOUR HOME A HANGOUT. CALL, TEXT, OR REACH OUT TO THEM RIGHT NOW.

BE THERE, DAD. BE AN AWESOME GRANDPA.

TEACH THEM HOW TO LOVE.

TEACH THEM HOW TO BE LOVED.

The DAD MANIFESTO

52 THINGS FOR FOREVER FATHERS TO NEVER FORGET

The Dad Manifesto © 2014
Words by Jay Payleitner.
Author/Speaker. JayPayleitner.com
Design by Chad Spohn, redletter.com

QUIT SMOKING.

*He must manage his own family well and
see that his children obey him, and he must
do so in a manner worthy of full respect.*

1 TIMOTHY 3:4

You can't tell your kids to *not* smoke if *you* smoke. Well you *can*, but it will have little impact. One thing kids can spot a mile away is a hypocrite.

You're not one of those dads, are you? The kind who curses, frequents every tavern in town, mocks religion, and then blames someone else when his kid lives a life marked by profanity, overindulgence, and godlessness.

Of course you're not. But children who watch Dad make bad decisions will make bad decisions. Kids who endure ongoing criticism will learn to malign others. Kids who watch Dad mope and whine will be mopers and whiners.

A better choice might be to demonstrate integrity, self-discipline, generosity, and gentleness. In other words, imagine the character traits you wish for your kids as they reach adulthood. And do those.

STOP AND CATCH THE FIREFLIES. LAUGH WITH THEM. CRY WITH THEM. GIVE NOOGIES.

ANSWER THEIR QUESTIONS WITH QUESTIONS.

DON'T CURSE THE TRAIN, COUNT THE CARS.

SPY ON YOUR KIDS. BUY A UNICYCLE.

SNUGGLE. RESPECT THEIR MOM.

LAUGH OVER SPILT MILK. QUIT SMOKING.

RESPOND TO ANY CRISIS, "I LOVE YOU. IT'LL BE OKAY. WE'LL GET THROUGH THIS TOGETHER."

HOLD YOUR BABY. TUCK IN. SAY BEDTIME PRAYERS.

RAKE LEAVES TOGETHER.

STOP RAKING TO WATCH THE GEESE FLY SOUTH IN "V" FORMATION.

IGNORE THE STICKBALL DENTS ON THE GARAGE DOOR.

WAKE YOUR KID FOR A LUNAR ECLIPSE. MAKE STILTS.

SUDDENLY YOUR 8-YEAR-OLD IS LOOKING YOU IN THE EYE.

QUIT GOLF. OR PATIENTLY TEACH THEM TO PLAY GOLF.

TEACH ROCK/PAPER/SCISSORS. TELL KNOCK-KNOCK JOKES. GIVE HORSEY RIDES.

PLAY H-O-R-S-E.

DON'T LET THEM WIN. THEY'LL BEAT YOU FAIR AND SQUARE SOON ENOUGH.

KISS YOUR WIFE IN THE KITCHEN.

DON'T BE THE JERK IN THE STANDS.

EARN THE RIGHT TO SAY WHAT NEEDS TO BE SAID.

CHAPERONE A SCHOOL DANCE.

CHAT OVER WAFFLES.

STOP AT HISTORICAL MARKERS. CUDDLE.

SKIP ROCKS. ALWAYS HAVE A CLEAN HANDKERCHIEF.

The DAD MANIFESTO
52 THINGS FOR FOREVER FATHERS TO NEVER FORGET

VOLUNTEER AT THEIR SCHOOL OR YOUTH GROUP.

Love you WRITE "LOVE YOU" ON A STICKY NOTE. APOLOGIZE

KEEP PROMISES. SOMETIMES SAY NO. WHEN YOU MESS UP.

RESCUE THEM AT THE TOP OF ANY SLIPPERY SLOPE.

MAKE TIME FOR THEM. THEY'LL MAKE TIME FOR YOU LATER. CARRY RECENT PHOTOS ON YOUR SMARTPHONE.

BE AMAZED WHEN THEY BRING YOU A BUG, DANDELION, OR SHINY ROCK.

MAKE YOUR HOME A HANGOUT.

CALL, TEXT, OR REACH OUT TO THEM RIGHT NOW.

BE THERE, DAD. BE AN AWESOME GRANDPA.

TEACH THEM HOW TO LOVE.

TEACH THEM HOW TO BE LOVED.

LAUGH OVER SPILT MILK.

*Fathers, do not exasperate your children;
instead, bring them up in the training
and instruction of the Lord.*

EPHESIANS 6:4

Your youngster already feels bad. Why pile on? Yelling will not improve the situation. Yelling will only exasperate your children. When the milk glass tumbles, your best course of action is to throw napkins at the spill and keep repeating, "No problem. No problem."

After addressing the immediate crisis, consider the next course of action. Maybe buy less slippery milk glasses. Pour smaller portions. Without too much fanfare, keep a roll of paper towels within reach. Please don't make your seven-year-old revert to using a sippy cup. Let them know that accidents happen but that you also expect them to be a little more careful.

If your child acts with intent and maliciousness, that's another story. But accidents *do* happen, and the tone you set will help your kids learn from their mistakes.

STOP AND CATCH THE FIREFLIES. LAUGH WITH THEM. CRY WITH THEM. GIVE NOOGIES.

ANSWER THEIR QUESTIONS WITH QUESTIONS. DON'T CURSE THE TRAIN, COUNT THE CARS.

SPY ON YOUR KIDS. BUY A UNICYCLE.

SNUGGLE. RESPECT THEIR MOM.

LAUGH OVER SPILT MILK. QUIT SMOKING.

RESPOND TO ANY CRISIS, "I LOVE YOU. IT'LL BE OKAY. WE'LL GET THROUGH THIS TOGETHER."

HOLD YOUR BABY. TUCK IN. SAY BEDTIME PRAYERS.

RAKE LEAVES TOGETHER. STOP RACING TO WATCH THE GEESE FLY SOUTH IN "V" FORMATION.

IGNORE THE STICKBALL DENTS ON THE GARAGE DOOR.

WAKE YOUR KID FOR A LUNAR ECLIPSE. MAKE STILTS. SUDDENLY YOUR 8-YEAR-OLD IS LOOKING YOU IN THE EYE.

QUIT GOLF. OR PATIENTLY TEACH THEM TO PLAY GOLF.

TEACH ROCK/PAPER/SCISSORS. TELL KNOCK-KNOCK JOKES. GIVE HORSEY RIDES.

PLAY H-O-R-S-E. DON'T LET THEM WIN. THEY'LL BEAT YOU FAIR AND SQUARE SOON ENOUGH.

KISS YOUR WIFE IN THE KITCHEN. DON'T BE THE JERK IN THE STANDS. CHAPERONE A SCHOOL DANCE.

EARN THE RIGHT TO SAY WHAT NEEDS TO BE SAID.

CHAT OVER WAFFLES.

STOP AT HISTORICAL MARKERS.

CUDDLE.

SKIP ROCKS. ALWAYS HAVE A CLEAN HANDKERCHIEF.

VOLUNTEER AT THEIR SCHOOL OR YOUTH GROUP.

WRITE "LOVE YOU" ON A STICKY NOTE. APOLOGIZE

KEEP PROMISES. SOMETIMES SAY NO. WHEN YOU MESS UP.

RESCUE THEM AT THE TOP OF ANY SLIPPERY SLOPE.

MAKE TIME FOR THEM. CARRY RECENT PHOTOS THEY'LL MAKE TIME FOR YOU LATER. ON YOUR SMARTPHONE.

BE AMAZED WHEN THEY BRING YOU A BUG, DANDELION, OR SHINY ROCK.

MAKE YOUR HOME A HANGOUT. CALL, TEXT, OR REACH OUT TO THEM RIGHT NOW.

BE THERE, DAD. BE AN AWESOME GRANDPA.

TEACH THEM HOW TO LOVE. TEACH THEM HOW TO BE LOVED.

The Dad Manifesto
52 THINGS FOR FOREVER FATHERS TO NEVER FORGET

The Dad Manifesto © 2014
Words By Jay Payleitner.
AuthorSpeaker, jaypayleitner.com
Design by Rex John, rexjohn.com

RESPOND TO ANY CRISIS, "I LOVE YOU. IT'LL BE OKAY. WE'LL GET THROUGH THIS TOGETHER."

The righteous cry out, and the LORD hears them; he delivers them from all their troubles. The LORD is close to the brokenhearted and saves those who are crushed in spirit.

PSALM 34:17-18

When bad stuff happens, you want your kids to come to you. Believe it or not, you want that phone call. "Dad, I wrecked the car." "Dad, I'm dropping out of school." "Dad, I'm in jail." "Dad, I'm pregnant." "Dad, my girlfriend is pregnant."

Your kids need to know Dad will help make bad things better. There will still be consequences. They're not "off the hook." But they know—without a doubt—that your attitude toward them will always be, "I love you. It'll be okay. We'll get through this together." Say it out loud, even now. That needs to be the attitude of your heart.

When life hits the fan, you want your kids coming to you, because the world does not love them. The world is broken. And the world will give them bad advice.

HOLD YOUR BABY.

For you created my inmost being; you knit me together in my mother's womb. I praise you because I am fearfully and wonderfully made; your works are wonderful, I know that full well. My frame was not hidden from you when I was made in the secret place.

PSALM 139:13-15

Over several years, we welcomed ten foster babies into our home. Mostly newborns. Some had been exposed to cocaine in their mother's womb, which meant they were essentially recovering addicts. I will never forget watching Rita and my five kids hold those precious infants while they endured seizures and withdrawal tremors.

The good news is that love is the most powerful force in the universe. Swaddling, rocking, and nuzzling from my family literally loved the residual cocaine right out of those babies. It was a true victory for all involved. Those rescued boys and girls we've kept track of are doing very well.

So, Dad. If being swaddled and rocked can heal a newborn of prenatal cocaine exposure, imagine what it does for healthy babies.

STOP AND CATCH THE FIREFLIES. LAUGH WITH THEM. CRY WITH THEM. GIVE NOOGIES.

ANSWER THEIR QUESTIONS WITH QUESTIONS. DON'T CURSE THE TRAIN, COUNT THE CARS.

SPY ON YOUR KIDS. BUY A UNICYCLE.

SNUGGLE. RESPECT THEIR MOM.

LAUGH OVER SPILT MILK. QUIT SMOKING.

RESPOND TO ANY CRISIS, "I LOVE YOU. IT'LL BE OKAY. WE'LL GET THROUGH THIS TOGETHER."

HOLD YOUR BABY. **TUCK IN.** SAY BEDTIME PRAYERS.

RAKE LEAVES TOGETHER. STOP RAKING TO WATCH THE GEESE FLY SOUTH IN "V" FORMATION.

IGNORE THE STICKBALL DENTS ON THE GARAGE DOOR. MAKE STILTS.

WAKE YOUR KID FOR A LUNAR ECLIPSE. SUDDENLY YOUR 8-YEAR-OLD IS LOOKING YOU IN THE EYE.

QUIT GOLF. OR PATIENTLY TEACH THEM TO PLAY GOLF.

TEACH ROCK/PAPER/SCISSORS. TELL KNOCK-KNOCK JOKES. GIVE HORSEY RIDES.

PLAY H-O-R-S-E. DON'T LET THEM WIN. THEY'LL BEAT YOU FAIR AND SQUARE SOON ENOUGH.

KISS YOUR WIFE IN THE KITCHEN. DON'T BE THE JERK IN THE STANDS.

CHAPERONE A SCHOOL DANCE.

EARN THE RIGHT TO SAY WHAT NEEDS TO BE SAID.

CHAT OVER WAFFLES. STOP AT HISTORICAL MARKERS.

CUDDLE.

The DAD MANIFESTO
52 THINGS FOR FOREVER FATHERS TO NEVER FORGET

SKIP ROCKS. ALWAYS HAVE A CLEAN HANDKERCHIEF.

VOLUNTEER AT THEIR SCHOOL OR YOUTH GROUP.

WRITE "LOVE YOU" ON A STICKY NOTE. APOLOGIZE

KEEP PROMISES. SOMETIMES SAY NO. WHEN YOU MESS UP.

RESCUE THEM AT THE TOP OF ANY SLIPPERY SLOPE.

MAKE TIME FOR THEM. THEY'LL MAKE TIME FOR YOU LATER. CARRY RECENT PHOTOS ON YOUR SMARTPHONE.

BE AMAZED WHEN THEY BRING YOU A BUG, DANDELION, OR SHINY ROCK. MAKE YOUR HOME A HANGOUT. CALL, TEXT, OR REACH OUT TO THEM RIGHT NOW.

BE THERE, DAD. BE AN AWESOME GRANDPA.

TEACH THEM HOW TO LOVE.

TEACH THEM HOW TO BE LOVED.

TUCK IN.

My son, do not let wisdom and understanding out of your sight, preserve sound judgment and discretion. When you lie down, you will not be afraid; when you lie down, your sleep will be sweet.

PROVERBS 3:21,24

The last moments of the day are the absolute best time to enter your child's world and discover what's on their hearts and minds. The lights are dim. The house is quiet. Prayers are said. Words of love and encouragement come easily.

You get a chance to put perspective on whatever happened that day—the small victories and any frustrations that still linger. You find out about the bully or the new friend. Their fears and their aspirations.

Make tucking in a habit, and you'll be welcome in their bedroom every night for 18 years. Some nights it might be just two minutes. Some midnight conversations with an older teen might go for hours.

Best of all, you're setting the tone for a wonderful tomorrow and ensuring their dreams will be sweet.

STOP AND CATCH THE FIREFLIES. LAUGH WITH THEM. CRY WITH THEM. GIVE NOOGIES. ANSWER THEIR QUESTIONS WITH QUESTIONS. DON'T CURSE THE TRAIN, COUNT THE CARS. SPY ON YOUR KIDS. BUY A UNICYCLE. SNUGGLE. RESPECT THEIR MOM. LAUGH OVER SPILT MILK. QUIT SMOKING. RESPOND TO ANY CRISIS, "I LOVE YOU. IT'LL BE OKAY. WE'LL GET THROUGH THIS TOGETHER." HOLD YOUR BABY. TUCK IN. SAY BEDTIME PRAYERS. RAKE LEAVES TOGETHER. STOP RAKING TO WATCH THE GEESE FLY SOUTH IN "V" FORMATION. IGNORE THE STICKBALL DENTS ON THE GARAGE DOOR. WAKE YOUR KID FOR A LUNAR ECLIPSE. MAKE STILTS. SUDDENLY YOUR 8-YEAR-OLD IS LOOKING YOU IN THE EYE. QUIT GOLF. OR PATIENTLY TEACH THEM TO PLAY GOLF. TEACH ROCK/PAPER/SCISSORS. TELL KNOCK-KNOCK JOKES. GIVE HORSEY RIDES. PLAY H-O-R-S-E. DON'T LET THEM WIN. THEY'LL BEAT YOU FAIR AND SQUARE SOON ENOUGH. KISS YOUR WIFE IN THE KITCHEN. DON'T BE THE JERK IN THE STANDS. CHAPERONE A SCHOOL DANCE. EARN THE RIGHT TO SAY WHAT NEEDS TO BE SAID. CHAT OVER WAFFLES. STOP AT HISTORICAL MARKERS. CUDDLE. SKIP ROCKS. ALWAYS HAVE A CLEAN HANDKERCHIEF. VOLUNTEER AT THEIR SCHOOL OR YOUTH GROUP. WRITE "LOVE YOU" ON A STICKY NOTE. APOLOGIZE KEEP PROMISES. SOMETIMES SAY NO. WHEN YOU MESS UP. RESCUE THEM AT THE TOP OF ANY SLIPPERY SLOPE. MAKE TIME FOR THEM. THEY'LL MAKE TIME FOR YOU LATER. CARRY RECENT PHOTOS ON YOUR SMARTPHONE. BE AMAZED WHEN THEY BRING YOU A BUG, DANDELION, OR SHINY ROCK. MAKE YOUR HOME A HANGOUT. CALL, TEXT, OR REACH OUT TO THEM RIGHT NOW. BE THERE, DAD. BE AN AWESOME GRANDPA. TEACH THEM HOW TO LOVE. TEACH THEM HOW TO BE LOVED.

The DAD MANIFESTO
52 THINGS FOR FOREVER FATHERS TO NEVER FORGET

The Dad Manifesto © 2014
Words by Jay Payleitner,
Author/Speaker. jaypayleitner.com
Design by Ryan Hill. ryandhill.com

SAY BEDTIME PRAYERS.

*Therefore let us draw near with confidence
to the throne of grace, so that we may receive
mercy and find grace to help in time of need.*

HEBREWS 4:16 NASB

Praying at bedtime should be a routine. But the prayer itself is not routine at all. See if you can find a new reason each night to give glory, give thanks, and ask for God's intervention. Tell your child that God knows their every need but still loves to hear their heartfelt words. And please don't include any of that "if I should die before I wake" imagery.

When they're little, keep it short and sweet. Nothing scary or ominous. As they get older, stretch those prayers. Go a bit longer. Pray for events and people outside your family. Add your own personal concerns. Encourage them to add their own voice. Maybe even keep a prayer log to record answered prayer. Your own faith will grow as God answers your children's sincere, trusting prayers.

STOP AND CATCH THE FIREFLIES. LAUGH WITH THEM. CRY WITH THEM. GIVE NOOGIES.

ANSWER THEIR QUESTIONS WITH QUESTIONS.

DON'T CURSE THE TRAIN, COUNT THE CARS.

SPY ON YOUR KIDS. BUY A UNICYCLE.

SNUGGLE. RESPECT THEIR MOM.

LAUGH OVER SPILT MILK. QUIT SMOKING.

RESPOND TO ANY CRISIS, "I LOVE YOU. IT'LL BE OKAY. WE'LL GET THROUGH THIS TOGETHER."

HOLD YOUR BABY. TUCK IN. SAY BEDTIME PRAYERS. RAKE LEAVES TOGETHER. STOP RAKING TO WATCH THE GEESE FLY SOUTH IN "V" FORMATION.

IGNORE THE STICKBALL DENTS ON THE GARAGE DOOR. MAKE STILTS.

WAKE YOUR KID FOR A LUNAR ECLIPSE. SUDDENLY YOUR 8-YEAR-OLD IS LOOKING YOU IN THE EYE.

QUIT GOLF. OR PATIENTLY TEACH THEM TO PLAY GOLF

TEACH ROCK/PAPER/SCISSORS. TELL KNOCK-KNOCK JOKES. GIVE HORSEY RIDES.

PLAY H-O-R-S-E. DON'T LET THEM WIN. THEY'LL BEAT YOU FAIR AND SQUARE SOON ENOUGH.

KISS YOUR WIFE IN THE KITCHEN.

DON'T BE THE JERK IN THE STANDS.

CHAPERONE A SCHOOL DANCE.

EARN THE RIGHT TO SAY WHAT NEEDS TO BE SAID.

CHAT OVER WAFFLES. STOP AT HISTORICAL MARKERS.

CUDDLE.

SKIP ROCKS. ALWAYS HAVE A CLEAN HANDKERCHIEF.

VOLUNTEER AT THEIR SCHOOL OR YOUTH GROUP.

WRITE "LOVE YOU" ON A STICKY NOTE. APOLOGIZE

KEEP PROMISES. SOMETIMES SAY NO. WHEN YOU MESS UP.

RESCUE THEM AT THE TOP OF ANY SLIPPERY SLOPE.

MAKE TIME FOR THEM. THEY'LL MAKE TIME FOR YOU LATER. CARRY RECENT PHOTOS ON YOUR SMARTPHONE.

BE AMAZED WHEN THEY BRING YOU A BUG, DANDELION, OR SHINY ROCK.

MAKE YOUR HOME A HANGOUT. CALL, TEXT, OR REACH OUT TO THEM RIGHT NOW.

BE THERE, DAD. BE AN AWESOME GRANDPA.

TEACH THEM HOW TO LOVE. TEACH THEM HOW TO BE LOVED.

The DAD MANIFESTO

52 THINGS FOR FOREVER FATHERS TO NEVER FORGET

The Dad Manifesto © 2014
words by Jay Payleitner
Author/speaker. jaypayleitner.com
Design by Rex Bohn. rexbohn.com

RAKE LEAVES TOGETHER.

*Whatever you do, do your work heartily,
as for the Lord rather than for men.*
COLOSSIANS 3:23 NASB

As kids get older, they need to be responsible for much of their own upkeep—their own laundry, getting themselves up and out the door, making their beds, and so on.

On top of that, they need to do regular chores for the common good. Setting the table, washing dishes, taking out the trash, mowing the lawn, sweeping the porch. Whatever works for your family.

Then there are the occasional seasonal jobs you all tackle together. Raking leaves, shoveling snow, mending fences, washing the car, planting the garden, spring-cleaning, painting the shed. Think of it as family teamwork. Make sure every member of the family pitches in with assignments that fit their skill level—just challenging enough.

The family that sweats together, sticks together. You can quote me on that.

STOP AND CATCH THE FIREFLIES. LAUGH WITH THEM. CRY WITH THEM. GIVE NOOGIES.

ANSWER THEIR QUESTIONS WITH QUESTIONS. DON'T CURSE THE TRAIN, COUNT THE CARS.

SPY ON YOUR KIDS. BUY A UNICYCLE.

SNUGGLE. RESPECT THEIR MOM.

LAUGH OVER SPILT MILK. QUIT SMOKING.

RESPOND TO ANY CRISIS, "I LOVE YOU. IT'LL BE OKAY. WE'LL GET THROUGH THIS TOGETHER."

HOLD YOUR BABY. TUCK IN. SAY BEDTIME PRAYERS. RAKE LEAVES TOGETHER. STOP RAKING TO WATCH THE GEESE FLY SOUTH IN 'V' FORMATION.

IGNORE THE STICKBALL DENTS ON THE GARAGE DOOR. MAKE STILTS.

WAKE YOUR KID FOR A LUNAR ECLIPSE. SUDDENLY YOUR 8-YEAR-OLD IS LOOKING YOU IN THE EYE.

QUIT GOLF. OR PATIENTLY TEACH THEM TO PLAY GOLF.

TEACH ROCK/PAPER/SCISSORS. TELL KNOCK-KNOCK JOKES. GIVE HORSEY RIDES.

PLAY H-O-R-S-E. DON'T LET THEM WIN. THEY'LL BEAT YOU FAIR AND SQUARE SOON ENOUGH.

The DAD MANIFESTO

52 THINGS FOR FOREVER FATHERS TO NEVER FORGET

KISS YOUR WIFE IN THE KITCHEN. DON'T BE THE JERK IN THE STANDS. CHAPERONE A SCHOOL DANCE.

EARN THE RIGHT TO SAY WHAT NEEDS TO BE SAID.

CHAT OVER WAFFLES.

STOP AT HISTORICAL MARKERS. CUDDLE.

SKIP ROCKS. ALWAYS HAVE A CLEAN HANDKERCHIEF.

VOLUNTEER AT THEIR SCHOOL OR YOUTH GROUP.

WRITE "LOVE YOU" ON A STICKY NOTE. APOLOGIZE

KEEP PROMISES. SOMETIMES SAY NO. WHEN YOU MESS UP.

RESCUE THEM AT THE TOP OF ANY SLIPPERY SLOPE.

MAKE TIME FOR THEM. THEY'LL MAKE TIME FOR YOU LATER. CARRY RECENT PHOTOS ON YOUR SMARTPHONE.

BE AMAZED WHEN THEY BRING YOU A BUG, DANDELION, OR SHINY ROCK. MAKE YOUR HOME A HANGOUT. CALL, TEXT, OR REACH OUT TO THEM RIGHT NOW.

BE THERE, DAD. BE AN AWESOME GRANDPA.

TEACH THEM HOW TO LOVE.

TEACH THEM HOW TO BE LOVED.

The Dad Manifesto © 2013. Words by Jay Payleitner. Artwork/Quotes: jaypayleitner.com. Design by Dog Eared, eyekymm.com

STOP RAKING TO WATCH THE GEESE FLY SOUTH IN 'V' FORMATION.

Look at the birds of the air; they do not sow
or reap or store away in barns, and yet
your heavenly Father feeds them. Are you
not much more valuable than they?

MATTHEW 6:26

One of the great joys of working together as a family is when work stops. For a well-earned break. For lunch. Because the sun is setting. Or because the job is finished. Applause and appreciation all around.

The best kind of breaks happen naturally. When geese fly over, you get to stop and ponder the reason for the "V" formation. (Ornithologists suggest it's for navigation and/or to minimize wind resistance.) When shoveling snow, stop and make snow angels. When washing the car, spin a bucket over your head and demonstrate centrifugal force. When cleaning the attic, stop and share memories from any box marked "Keepsakes."

By introducing an element of joy into a family project, you're establishing an attitude about work that will serve your children well for years to come.

STOP AND CATCH THE FIREFLIES.  LAUGH WITH THEM. CRY WITH THEM. GIVE NOOGIES.

ANSWER THEIR QUESTIONS WITH QUESTIONS.

DON'T CURSE THE TRAIN, COUNT THE CARS.

SPY ON YOUR KIDS. BUY A UNICYCLE.

SNUGGLE. RESPECT THEIR MOM.

LAUGH OVER SPILT MILK. QUIT SMOKING.

RESPOND TO ANY CRISIS, "I LOVE YOU. IT'LL BE OKAY. WE'LL GET THROUGH THIS TOGETHER."

HOLD YOUR BABY. TUCK IN. SAY BEDTIME PRAYERS.

RAKE LEAVES TOGETHER.

STOP RAKING TO WATCH THE GEESE FLY SOUTH IN "V" FORMATION.

IGNORE THE STICKBALL DENTS ON THE GARAGE DOOR.

WAKE YOUR KID FOR A LUNAR ECLIPSE. MAKE STILTS.

SUDDENLY YOUR 8-YEAR-OLD IS LOOKING YOU IN THE EYE.

QUIT GOLF. OR PATIENTLY TEACH THEM TO PLAY GOLF.

TEACH ROCK/PAPER/SCISSORS. TELL KNOCK-KNOCK JOKES. GIVE HORSEY RIDES.

PLAY H-O-R-S-E.

DON'T LET THEM WIN. THEY'LL BEAT YOU FAIR AND SQUARE SOON ENOUGH.

The DAD MANIFESTO
52 THINGS FOR FOREVER FATHERS TO NEVER FORGET

KISS YOUR WIFE IN THE KITCHEN.

DON'T BE THE JERK IN THE STANDS.

CHAPERONE A SCHOOL DANCE.

EARN THE RIGHT TO SAY WHAT NEEDS TO BE SAID.

CHAT OVER WAFFLES.

STOP AT HISTORICAL MARKERS.

CUDDLE.

SKIP ROCKS. ALWAYS HAVE A CLEAN HANDKERCHIEF.

VOLUNTEER AT THEIR SCHOOL OR YOUTH GROUP.

WRITE "LOVE YOU" ON A STICKY NOTE. APOLOGIZE

KEEP PROMISES. SOMETIMES SAY NO. WHEN YOU MESS UP.

RESCUE THEM AT THE TOP OF ANY SLIPPERY SLOPE.

MAKE TIME FOR THEM. CARRY RECENT PHOTOS ON YOUR SMARTPHONE.

THEY'LL MAKE TIME FOR YOU LATER.

BE AMAZED WHEN THEY BRING YOU A BUG, DANDELION, OR SHINY ROCK.

MAKE YOUR HOME A HANGOUT.

CALL, TEXT, OR REACH OUT TO THEM RIGHT NOW.

BE THERE, DAD. BE AN AWESOME GRANDPA.

TEACH THEM HOW TO LOVE.

TEACH THEM HOW TO BE LOVED.

The Dad Manifesto © 2014
Words by Jay Payleitner,
Author/Speaker, jaypayleitner.com
Design by Don Solsa, roxbute.com

IGNORE THE STICKBALL DENTS ON THE GARAGE DOOR.

*Fools vent their anger, but the
wise quietly hold it back.*
PROVERBS 29:11 NLT

Pulling up to my driveway, I saw it instantly. My son, Isaac, and his three college buddies had gashed my new $1200 garage door. Not with the Wiffle balls, but with the broom handle on their backswing.

At another time or place, I might have raged. But I did not. Somehow God helped me see the beauty of the moment. These young men weren't pounding beers or playing creepy video games. They were playing the time-honored game of stickball. In my driveway. What a privilege. Instead of pointing out how Isaac had let me down, I had the good sense to smile and say, "Swing away."

Dad, I pray you have the same loving response when your door is dented. Trust me, there's plenty of time to re-sod, re-screen, and re-carpet after the kids are gone.

STOP AND CATCH THE FIREFLIES.
LAUGH WITH THEM. CRY WITH THEM.
GIVE NOOGIES.
ANSWER THEIR QUESTIONS WITH QUESTIONS.
DON'T CURSE THE TRAIN, COUNT THE CARS.
SPY ON YOUR KIDS. BUY A UNICYCLE.
SNUGGLE. RESPECT THEIR MOM.
LAUGH OVER SPILT MILK. QUIT SMOKING.
RESPOND TO ANY CRISIS, "I LOVE YOU. IT'LL BE OKAY. WE'LL GET THROUGH THIS TOGETHER."
HOLD YOUR BABY. TUCK IN. SAY BEDTIME PRAYERS.
RAKE LEAVES TOGETHER.
STOP RAKING TO WATCH THE GEESE FLY SOUTH IN "V" FORMATION.
IGNORE THE STICKBALL DENTS ON THE GARAGE DOOR.
MAKE STILTS.
WAKE YOUR KID FOR A LUNAR ECLIPSE.
SUDDENLY YOUR 8-YEAR-OLD IS LOOKING YOU IN THE EYE.
QUIT GOLF. OR PATIENTLY TEACH THEM TO PLAY GOLF.
TEACH ROCK/PAPER/SCISSORS. TELL KNOCK-KNOCK JOKES. GIVE HORSEY RIDES.
PLAY H-O-R-S-E.
DON'T LET THEM WIN. THEY'LL BEAT YOU FAIR AND SQUARE SOON ENOUGH.
KISS YOUR WIFE IN THE KITCHEN.
DON'T BE THE JERK IN THE STANDS.
CHAPERONE A SCHOOL DANCE.

The DAD MANIFESTO
52 THINGS FOR FOREVER FATHERS TO NEVER FORGET

EARN THE RIGHT TO SAY WHAT NEEDS TO BE SAID.
CHAT OVER WAFFLES.
STOP AT HISTORICAL MARKERS.
CUDDLE.
SKIP ROCKS.
ALWAYS HAVE A CLEAN HANDKERCHIEF.
VOLUNTEER AT THEIR SCHOOL OR YOUTH GROUP.
WRITE "LOVE YOU" ON A STICKY NOTE.
APOLOGIZE
KEEP PROMISES. SOMETIMES SAY NO. WHEN YOU MESS UP.
RESCUE THEM AT THE TOP OF ANY SLIPPERY SLOPE.
MAKE TIME FOR THEM. CARRY RECENT PHOTOS
THEY'LL MAKE TIME FOR YOU LATER. ON YOUR SMARTPHONE.
BE AMAZED MAKE YOUR HOME A HANGOUT.
WHEN THEY BRING YOU A BUG, DANDELION, OR SHINY ROCK.
CALL, TEXT, OR REACH OUT TO THEM RIGHT NOW.
BE THERE, DAD. BE AN AWESOME GRANDPA.
TEACH THEM HOW TO LOVE.
TEACH THEM HOW TO BE LOVED.

MAKE STILTS.

The LORD makes firm the steps of the one who delights in him; though he may stumble, he will not fall, for the LORD upholds him with his hand.

PSALM 37:23-24

Got a free weekend afternoon? Instead of watching golf or NASCAR for three hours, invest that time in your grade-school son or daughter. Even if you don't have an organized workshop, you can still slap a few pieces of wood together, right? Don't make a birdhouse that hangs passively waiting for a new tenant. Don't make some knickknack that just sits on a shelf.

Go online, search for "making stilts," and then just do it. You may or may not need a quick trip to the lumberyard. But that's part of the process.

Let them do much of the work. You'll watch them learn a new skill, grow tall, stumble, get back up, and gain new confidence. All in one afternoon.

STOP AND CATCH THE FIREFLIES. LAUGH WITH THEM. CRY WITH THEM. GIVE NOOGIES.

ANSWER THEIR QUESTIONS WITH QUESTIONS.

DON'T CURSE THE TRAIN, COUNT THE CARS.

SPY ON YOUR KIDS. BUY A UNICYCLE.

SNUGGLE. RESPECT THEIR MOM.

LAUGH OVER SPILT MILK. QUIT SMOKING.

RESPOND TO ANY CRISIS, "I LOVE YOU. IT'LL BE OKAY. WE'LL GET THROUGH THIS TOGETHER."

HOLD YOUR BABY. TUCK IN. SAY BEDTIME PRAYERS.

RAKE LEAVES TOGETHER.

STOP RAKING TO WATCH THE GEESE FLY SOUTH IN "V" FORMATION.

IGNORE THE STICKBALL DENTS ON THE GARAGE DOOR. MAKE STILTS.

WAKE YOUR KID FOR A LUNAR ECLIPSE.

SUDDENLY YOUR 8-YEAR-OLD IS LOOKING YOU IN THE EYE.

QUIT GOLF. OR PATIENTLY TEACH THEM TO PLAY GOLF.

TEACH ROCK/PAPER/SCISSORS. TELL KNOCK-KNOCK JOKES. GIVE HORSEY RIDES.

PLAY H-O-R-S-E.

DON'T LET THEM WIN, THEY'LL BEAT YOU FAIR AND SQUARE SOON ENOUGH.

EARN THE RIGHT TO SAY WHAT NEEDS TO BE SAID.

CHAT OVER WAFFLES.

STOP AT HISTORICAL MARKERS.

The DAD MANIFESTO

52 THINGS FOR FOREVER FATHERS TO NEVER FORGET

KISS YOUR WIFE IN THE KITCHEN.

DON'T BE THE JERK IN THE STANDS.

CHAPERONE A SCHOOL DANCE.

CUDDLE.

SKIP ROCKS. ALWAYS HAVE A CLEAN HANDKERCHIEF.

VOLUNTEER AT THEIR SCHOOL OR YOUTH GROUP.

Love you WRITE "LOVE YOU" ON A STICKY NOTE. APOLOGIZE

KEEP PROMISES. SOMETIMES SAY NO. WHEN YOU MESS UP.

RESCUE THEM AT THE TOP OF ANY SLIPPERY SLOPE.

MAKE TIME FOR THEM. THEY'LL MAKE TIME FOR YOU LATER. CARRY RECENT PHOTOS ON YOUR SMARTPHONE.

BE AMAZED WHEN THEY BRING YOU A BUG, DANDELION, OR SHINY ROCK. MAKE YOUR HOME A HANGOUT.

CALL, TEXT, OR REACH OUT TO THEM RIGHT NOW.

BE THERE, DAD. BE AN AWESOME GRANDPA.

TEACH THEM HOW TO LOVE.

TEACH THEM HOW TO BE LOVED.

The Dad Manifesto © 2014 Jay K. Payleitner. Author/Speaker. JayPayleitner.com Design by Dugan Design Group. dugandesign.com

SUDDENLY YOUR 8-YEAR-OLD IS LOOKING YOU IN THE EYE.

*Be on guard; then you will not be carried away by
the errors of these wicked people and lose your own
secure footing. Rather, you must grow in the grace
and knowledge of our Lord and Savior Jesus Christ.*

2 PETER 3:17-18 NLT

Our kids are kids. And we need to accept the idea that
they will make mistakes. They will fail. They will fall.
For years, they are going to need our help, guidance, and
supervision.

However, we also need to see them as future adults.
When they stumble, we need to choose our response
carefully. Sometimes we rescue. Sometimes we allow
them to suffer minor consequences. Sometimes we let
them hit bottom and work it out for themselves.

Absolutely, we should help them find and establish
secure footing. Then we need to step back and let them
practice being an adult. The world will continue trying to
knock them off any firm foundation, but if it's built with
godly principles, they will keep their balance.

WAKE YOUR KID FOR A LUNAR ECLIPSE.

When I consider your heavens, the work of your fingers, the moon and the stars, which you have set in place, what is mankind that you are mindful of them, human beings that you care for them?

PSALM 8:3-4

Quiz: On a school night, you hear the sky will be clear for a dramatic view of a rare lunar eclipse at 2 a.m. Does your child's mom want you to wake your second grader? Of course not. But should you? Absolutely.

The next day, when the teacher asks why they're slightly groggy, your son or daughter will simply say, "My dad got me up for the lunar eclipse." The teacher will smile and shake her head. All the other kids will be jealous. And your child will remember that event forever.

By the way, as the two of you look up into that night sky, don't forget to mention who placed the stars and remind your precious child you love them to the moon and back. And so does that Creator God.

STOP AND CATCH THE FIREFLIES.

LAUGH WITH THEM. CRY WITH THEM. GIVE NOOGIES.

ANSWER THEIR QUESTIONS WITH QUESTIONS.

DON'T CURSE THE TRAIN, COUNT THE CARS.

SPY ON YOUR KIDS. BUY A UNICYCLE.

SNUGGLE. RESPECT THEIR MOM.

LAUGH OVER SPILT MILK. QUIT SMOKING.

RESPOND TO ANY CRISIS, "I LOVE YOU. IT'LL BE OKAY. WE'LL GET THROUGH THIS TOGETHER."

HOLD YOUR BABY. TUCK IN. SAY BEDTIME PRAYERS.

RAKE LEAVES TOGETHER.

STOP RAKING TO WATCH THE GEESE FLY SOUTH IN "V" FORMATION.

IGNORE THE STICKBALL DENTS ON THE GARAGE DOOR. MAKE STILTS.

WAKE YOUR KID FOR A LUNAR ECLIPSE. SUDDENLY YOUR 8-YEAR-OLD IS LOOKING YOU IN THE EYE.

QUIT GOLF. OR PATIENTLY TEACH THEM TO PLAY GOLF.

TEACH ROCK/PAPER/SCISSORS. TELL KNOCK-KNOCK JOKES. GIVE HORSEY RIDES.

PLAY H-O-R-S-E.

DON'T LET THEM WIN. THEY'LL BEAT YOU FAIR AND SQUARE SOON ENOUGH.

EARN THE RIGHT TO SAY WHAT NEEDS TO BE SAID.

CHAT OVER WAFFLES.

STOP AT HISTORICAL MARKERS.

SKIP ROCKS.

The DAD MANIFESTO
52 THINGS FOR FOREVER FATHERS TO NEVER FORGET

KISS YOUR WIFE IN THE KITCHEN.

DON'T BE THE JERK IN THE STANDS.

CHAPERONE A SCHOOL DANCE.

CUDDLE.

ALWAYS HAVE A CLEAN HANDKERCHIEF.

VOLUNTEER AT THEIR SCHOOL OR YOUTH GROUP.

Love you WRITE "LOVE YOU" ON A STICKY NOTE. APOLOGIZE WHEN YOU MESS UP.

KEEP PROMISES. SOMETIMES SAY NO.

RESCUE THEM AT THE TOP OF ANY SLIPPERY SLOPE.

MAKE TIME FOR THEM. CARRY RECENT PHOTOS
THEY'LL MAKE TIME FOR YOU LATER. ON YOUR SMARTPHONE.

BE AMAZED MAKE YOUR HOME A HANGOUT.
WHEN THEY BRING YOU A BUG, CALL, TEXT, OR REACH OUT
DANDELION, OR SHINY ROCK. TO THEM RIGHT NOW.

BE THERE, DAD. BE AN AWESOME GRANDPA.

The Dad Manifesto © 2013
Words by Jay Payleitner.
Augus/Special: jaypayleitner.com
Design by Rob Eagar, rveitcho.com

TEACH THEM HOW TO LOVE.
TEACH THEM HOW TO BE LOVED.

22

QUIT GOLF.

*Fathers, do not exasperate your children,
so that they will not lose heart.*
COLOSSIANS 3:21 NASB

I'll never forget a young boy on my baseball team who had really sharpened his skills through the season. Unfortunately, his dad never saw him play. Our games were on weeknights, and that father traveled for work. (That happens sometimes and can't be avoided. I get that.)

When a rainout was rescheduled for Saturday, the boy was delighted. "Coach Payleitner, my dad can see me play!" I decided to start him at shortstop to show off for his dad. Saturday morning, the kid comes hanging his head. He says, "My dad... he can't come. He... he has to play golf."

Dad, for a season of life, *make your kids your hobby.* Set aside your own desires. Any extra time you have is *theirs.* And maybe even quit golf.

STOP AND CATCH THE FIREFLIES.

LAUGH WITH THEM. CRY WITH THEM.

GIVE NOOGIES.

ANSWER THEIR QUESTIONS WITH QUESTIONS.

DON'T CURSE THE TRAIN, COUNT THE CARS.

SPY ON YOUR KIDS. BUY A UNICYCLE.

SNUGGLE. RESPECT THEIR MOM.

LAUGH OVER SPILT MILK. QUIT SMOKING.

RESPOND TO ANY CRISIS: "I LOVE YOU. IT'LL BE OKAY. WE'LL GET THROUGH THIS TOGETHER."

HOLD YOUR BABY. TUCK IN. SAY BEDTIME PRAYERS.

RAKE LEAVES TOGETHER.

STOP RAKING TO WATCH THE GEESE FLY SOUTH IN "V" FORMATION.

IGNORE THE STICKBALL DENTS ON THE GARAGE DOOR.

WAKE YOUR KID FOR A LUNAR ECLIPSE. MAKE STILTS.

SUDDENLY YOUR 8-YEAR-OLD IS LOOKING YOU IN THE EYE.

QUIT GOLF. OR PATIENTLY TEACH THEM TO PLAY GOLF.

TEACH ROCK/PAPER/SCISSORS. TELL KNOCK-KNOCK JOKES. GIVE HORSEY RIDES.

PLAY H-O-R-S-E.

DON'T LET HIM WIN. THEY'LL BEAT YOU FAIR AND SQUARE SOON ENOUGH.

KISS YOUR WIFE IN THE KITCHEN.

DON'T BE THE JERK IN THE STANDS.

EARN THE RIGHT TO SAY WHAT NEEDS TO BE SAID.

CHAPERONE A SCHOOL DANCE.

CHAT OVER WAFFLES.

The DAD MANIFESTO

52 THINGS FOR FOREVER FATHERS TO NEVER FORGET

STOP AT HISTORICAL MARKERS.

CUDDLE.

SKIP ROCKS.

ALWAYS HAVE A CLEAN HANDKERCHIEF.

VOLUNTEER AT THEIR SCHOOL OR YOUTH GROUP.

Love you WRITE "LOVE YOU" ON A STICKY NOTE. APOLOGIZE

KEEP PROMISES. SOMETIMES SAY NO. WHEN YOU MESS UP.

RESCUE THEM AT THE TOP OF ANY SLIPPERY SLOPE.

MAKE TIME FOR THEM. THEY'LL MAKE TIME FOR YOU LATER. CARRY RECENT PHOTOS ON YOUR SMARTPHONE.

BE AMAZED WHEN THEY BRING YOU A BUG, DANDELION, OR SHINY ROCK. MAKE YOUR HOME A HANGOUT.

CALL, TEXT, OR REACH OUT TO THEM RIGHT NOW.

BE THERE, DAD. BE AN AWESOME GRANDPA.

TEACH THEM HOW TO LOVE.

TEACH THEM HOW TO BE LOVED.

The Dad Manifesto © 2014
Words by Jay Payleitner.
Author/Speaker: jaypayleitner.com
Design by Rex Bohn. rexbohn.com

23

OR PATIENTLY TEACH THEM TO PLAY GOLF.

*Train up a child in the way he should go, and
when he is old he will not depart from it.*
PROVERBS 22:6 NKJV

Be proactive about inviting your son or daughter into your world. Sure, it's easier to assemble that picnic table without their help. The trip to the hardware store is quicker if they don't tag along. A round of golf with your ten-year-old can be a little frustrating.

But in the long run, the benefits far outweigh any sacrifice. You are the best person to reveal the magical properties of a socket wrench to your child. Walking the aisles of a hardware store with Dad is like visiting a secret world. And being there when your kid makes par for the first time is something the two of you will remember forever. Plus, 20 years from now you may get a phone call: "Hey, Dad, want to play a round of golf this weekend?"

24

TEACH ROCK/PAPER/SCISSORS.

A youngster's heart is filled with foolishness,
but physical discipline will drive it far away.
PROVERBS 22:15 NLT

The random act of throwing a clenched fist, a flat palm, or a sideways peace sign gives any child a rare chance to beat their father fair and square.

But be warned. Teach a four-year-old to play rock/paper/scissors, and it will soon be a favorite pastime.

Now here's a secret you must never share with your child. When a new round begins, every kid between the age of four and nine will start by throwing "scissors." Guaranteed. So if you want to give them a momentary thrill of victory, throw "paper." On the other hand, if you are deciding who should do some minor chore, go ahead and throw "rock." You win, and they have to fetch the newspaper or empty the kitchen trash. Try it out today. And please don't reveal this secret.

25

TELL KNOCK-KNOCK JOKES.

The father of godly children has cause for joy.
What a pleasure to have children who are wise.

PROVERBS 23:24 NLT

Knock, knock. *Who's there?* Isabel. *Isabel who?* Isabel working? I had to knock.

Knock, knock. *Who's there?* Dwayne. *Dwayne who?* Dwayne the bathtub, I'm dwowning.

Knock, knock. *Who's there?* Lettuce. *Lettuce who?* Lettuce in, it's cold out here.

Knock, knock. *Who's there?* Radio. *Radio who?* Radio not, here I come.

Knock, knock. *Who's there?* Wooden shoe. *Wooden shoe who?* Wooden shoe like to know?

Knock, knock. *Who's there?* Boo. *Boo who?* It's only a joke—you don't have to cry.

Knock, knock. *Who's there?* Hatch. *Hatch who?* Gesundheit.

Knock, knock. *Who's there?* Little old lady. *Little old lady who?* Wow! I didn't know you could yodel.

STOP AND CATCH THE FIREFLIES. LAUGH WITH THEM. CRY WITH THEM. GIVE NOOGIES.

ANSWER THEIR QUESTIONS WITH QUESTIONS.

DON'T CURSE THE TRAIN, COUNT THE CARS.

SPY ON YOUR KIDS. BUY A UNICYCLE.

SNUGGLE. RESPECT THEIR MOM.

LAUGH OVER SPILT MILK. QUIT SMOKING.

RESPOND TO ANY CRISIS, "I LOVE YOU. IT'LL BE OKAY. WE'LL GET THROUGH THIS TOGETHER."

HOLD YOUR BABY. TUCK IN. SAY BEDTIME PRAYERS.

RAKE LEAVES TOGETHER.

STOP RAKING TO WATCH THE GEESE FLY SOUTH IN "V" FORMATION.

IGNORE THE STICKBALL DENTS ON THE GARAGE DOOR. MAKE STILTS.

WAKE YOUR KID FOR A LUNAR ECLIPSE.

SUDDENLY YOUR 8-YEAR-OLD IS LOOKING YOU IN THE EYE.

QUIT GOLF. OR PATIENTLY TEACH THEM TO PLAY GOLF.

TEACH ROCK/PAPER/SCISSORS. TELL KNOCK-KNOCK JOKES. GIVE HORSEY RIDES.

PLAY H-O-R-S-E.

DON'T LET THEM WIN. THEY'LL BEAT YOU FAIR AND SQUARE SOON ENOUGH.

EARN THE RIGHT TO SAY WHAT NEEDS TO BE SAID.

CHAT OVER WAFFLES.

STOP AT HISTORICAL MARKERS.

The DAD MANIFESTO

52 THINGS FOR FOREVER FATHERS TO NEVER FORGET

KISS YOUR WIFE IN THE KITCHEN.

DON'T BE THE JERK IN THE STANDS.

CHAPERONE A SCHOOL DANCE.

CUDDLE.

SKIP ROCKS. ALWAYS HAVE A CLEAN HANDKERCHIEF.

VOLUNTEER AT THEIR SCHOOL OR YOUTH GROUP.

Love you WRITE "LOVE YOU" ON A STICKY NOTE. APOLOGIZE

KEEP PROMISES. SOMETIMES SAY NO. WHEN YOU MESS UP.

RESCUE THEM AT THE TOP OF ANY SLIPPERY SLOPE.

MAKE TIME FOR THEM. CARRY RECENT PHOTOS

THEY'LL MAKE TIME FOR YOU LATER. ON YOUR SMARTPHONE.

BE AMAZED MAKE YOUR HOME A HANGOUT.

WHEN THEY BRING YOU A BUG, DANDELION, OR SHINY ROCK.

CALL, TEXT, OR REACH OUT TO THEM RIGHT NOW.

BE THERE, DAD. BE AN AWESOME GRANDPA.

TEACH THEM HOW TO LOVE.

TEACH THEM HOW TO BE LOVED.

The Dad Manifesto © 2014
words by Jay Payleitner.
Author/speaker. JayPayleitner.com
Design by Dan Mann. redbubbo.com

26

GIVE HORSEY RIDES.

*For where your treasure is, there
your heart will be also.*
MATTHEW 6:21

If you can swing it financially, you probably want to take your family to Disney World at least once. For the right age, the Magic Kingdom is indeed almost magic. But if you're talking about a three-year-old, I'm not so sure. You can plop them in a teacup or on a flying Dumbo. They will recognize the Pixar characters. But in general, my recommendation is to save the cash-grabbing theme parks for slightly older kids.

Instead, for toddlers, designate *yourself* as their favorite amusement park ride. Hoist them on your shoulders. Twirl them like a tilt-a-whirl. Let them dance on your shoes. And don't forget good old-fashioned horsey rides. Practice your neighs. Teach your little cowpoke to say giddyap. Do a little bucking bronco. Let them feed you carrots.

Save your money. Invest your heart. And watch your knees.

27

PLAY H-O-R-S-E.

*As iron sharpens iron, so one
person sharpens another.*
PROVERBS 27:17

You know how to play H-O-R-S-E, right? It's a driveway basketball game in which players take turns making similar shots. An easy layup. A hook shot from six feet out. A swish from the oil spot by the garage door. If you make it and the next player doesn't, he or she gets a letter. A player who gets five letters is eliminated.

H-O-R-S-E works because it's just competitive enough. No one is dripping sweat, sucking wind, or throwing elbows. Between shots you can sneak in a little meaningful conversation. Plus, you get to model the difference between respectful trash talk and the kind that is just plain mean. Same idea goes for batting cages, goalie practice, running pass routes, and any other sporting endeavor in which you can still keep up with your son or daughter.

DON'T LET THEM WIN.
THEY'LL BEAT YOU FAIR AND SQUARE SOON ENOUGH.

*The godly walk with integrity; blessed
are their children who follow them.*
PROVERBS 20:7 NLT

Never let your preteen beat you in driveway basketball.
Or checkers. Or Scrabble. Or Ping-Pong. Or anything that
requires skill, knowledge, and practice. Because in a few
years, they *will* beat you, and their hard-earned victory
will be ever so sweet.

There are exceptions to this rule. Allow your pre-
schooler to tackle you in knee football or pin you to the
carpet in family-room wrestling. They know Daddy is
bigger and stronger.

Allow your middle schooler to beat you in most video
games. They will anyway, so don't kill yourself trying to
be competitive. Their reflexes are faster, and they know
shortcuts and secrets you don't.

And on a rare occasion, if your 12-year-old has
been really working on their game, let them taste victory. Model how to lose graciously. And make sure you
soundly win the next few rounds.

STOP AND CATCH THE FIREFLIES.

LAUGH WITH THEM. CRY WITH THEM.

GIVE NOOGIES.

ANSWER THEIR QUESTIONS WITH QUESTIONS.

DON'T CURSE THE TRAIN, COUNT THE CARS.

SPY ON YOUR KIDS. BUY A UNICYCLE.

SNUGGLE. RESPECT THEIR MOM.

LAUGH OVER SPILT MILK. QUIT SMOKING.

RESPOND TO ANY CRISIS, "I LOVE YOU. IT'LL BE OKAY. WE'LL GET THROUGH THIS TOGETHER."

HOLD YOUR BABY. TUCK IN. SAY BEDTIME PRAYERS.

RAKE LEAVES TOGETHER.

STOP RAKING TO WATCH THE GEESE FLY SOUTH IN "V" FORMATION.

IGNORE THE STICKBALL DENTS ON THE GARAGE DOOR.

WAKE YOUR KID FOR A LUNAR ECLIPSE.

MAKE STILTS.

SUDDENLY YOUR 8-YEAR-OLD IS LOOKING YOU IN THE EYE.

QUIT GOLF. OR PATIENTLY TEACH THEM TO PLAY GOLF.

TEACH ROCK/PAPER/SCISSORS. TELL KNOCK-KNOCK JOKES. GIVE HORSEY RIDES.

PLAY H-O-R-S-E.

DON'T LET THEM WIN. THEY'LL BEAT YOU FAIR AND SQUARE SOON ENOUGH.

The DAD MANIFESTO

52 THINGS FOR FOREVER FATHERS TO NEVER FORGET

KISS YOUR WIFE IN THE KITCHEN.

DON'T BE THE JERK IN THE STANDS.

CHAPERONE A SCHOOL DANCE.

EARN THE RIGHT TO SAY WHAT NEEDS TO BE SAID.

CHAT OVER WAFFLES.

STOP AT HISTORICAL MARKERS.

CUDDLE.

SKIP ROCKS.

ALWAYS HAVE A CLEAN HANDKERCHIEF.

VOLUNTEER AT THEIR SCHOOL OR YOUTH GROUP.

Love you

WRITE "LOVE YOU" ON A STICKY NOTE.

APOLOGIZE

KEEP PROMISES. SOMETIMES SAY NO. WHEN YOU MESS UP.

RESCUE THEM AT THE TOP OF ANY SLIPPERY SLOPE.

MAKE TIME FOR THEM. CARRY RECENT PHOTOS

THEY'LL MAKE TIME FOR YOU LATER. ON YOUR SMARTPHONE.

BE AMAZED

MAKE YOUR HOME A HANGOUT.

WHEN THEY BRING YOU A BUG, DANDELION, OR SHINY ROCK.

CALL, TEXT, OR REACH OUT TO THEM RIGHT NOW.

BE THERE, DAD. BE AN AWESOME GRANDPA.

TEACH THEM HOW TO LOVE.

TEACH THEM HOW TO BE LOVED.

The Dad Manifesto © 2014
Words By Jay Payleitner
Author/Speaker, jaypayleitner.com
Design by Del Sams, rushmit.com

29

KISS YOUR WIFE IN THE KITCHEN.

Enjoy life with your wife, whom you love.
ECCLESIASTES 9:9

With marriages breaking up all around them, your kids need to know that Mom and Dad are committed to each to other and that marriage works.

So I recommend the kitchen make-out. It achieves three worthy objectives. It tells your bride you love her. It tells your kids you love their mom. It demonstrates that passion can happen in a committed, lifelong marriage relationship.

Most kisses your kids see on television are between couples that are not married. (At least not to each other.) Hollywood seems to think that after the wedding ceremony, the romance is gone. Well, I disagree. And so does God.

So kiss your bride in the kitchen. The goal is for your fourth grader to go, "Ewwww!" or your teenager to wisecrack, "Get a room!" That's a sure signal you're doing it right.

30

DON'T BE THE JERK IN THE STANDS.

Everyone should be quick to listen, slow to speak and slow to become angry, because human anger does not produce the righteousness that God desires.

JAMES 1:19-20

Over the years I did more than my share of stomping around sidelines, muttering under my breath, and yelling at umpires and referees. Looking back, I can't bear to think of the way I acted.

By the way, don't think for a moment your wife and kids are not horrified by your behavior. Let me assure you, they feel betrayed and embarrassed.

So how can a dad minimize or eliminate his jerk-in-the-stands behavior? Give your wife permission to nudge you if she senses your frustration building. Walk down to the end zone or foul pole. Give yourself a distraction. Volunteer to work the concession stand, video the action, work the chain gang at a football game, or be a linesman for soccer.

Or maybe pray away that demon and *enjoy* the game. What a concept.

31

CHAPERONE
A SCHOOL DANCE.

*When [Jesus's] parents saw him, they were astonished.
His mother said to him, "Son, why have you treated
us like this? Your father and I have been anxiously
searching for you." "Why were you searching for
me?" he asked. "Didn't you know I had to be in my
Father's house?"...But his mother treasured all
these things in her heart. And Jesus grew in wisdom
and stature, and in favor with God and man.*

LUKE 2:48-52

Sometimes kids want to do their own thing without
Mom and Dad around. So when you sign up to help with
the school dance, church event, or fund-raiser, here are
some strategies to consider. Stay in your assigned zone.
Don't embarrass them. Don't expect your child to hang
out with you. When your child's friends come to say hi,
don't interrogate them. The next day, don't analyze the
event. Just be glad you had a chance to enter their world.

One final note: Don't ask your child's permission
ahead of time. For obvious reasons, they'll say no. And
really, can you blame them?

32

EARN THE RIGHT TO SAY WHAT NEEDS TO BE SAID.

*Wise words bring approval, but fools
are destroyed by their own words.*
ECCLESIASTES 10:12 NLT

The title of "father" doesn't automatically mean your kids will listen to you. A dad can't demand respect—he can only earn it.

If you have a history of verbally trashing them or physically abusing them, what makes you think your children will listen to anything you have to say? They won't.

Thankfully, the opposite is also true. If your verbal interaction is affirming and your touch is always under control, you will be trustworthy. If you speak truth and listen to their side of the story before judging, your word will have value. If you listen to their fears and dreams without derision, they will ask for your wisdom and experience.

Show them respect, and they just might put down their phones, take out their earbuds, or stop texting long enough to hold a real conversation.

STOP AND CATCH THE FIREFLIES. LAUGH WITH THEM. CRY WITH THEM. GIVE NOOGIES.

ANSWER THEIR QUESTIONS WITH QUESTIONS. DON'T CURSE THE TRAIN, COUNT THE CARS.

SPY ON YOUR KIDS. BUY A UNICYCLE.

SNUGGLE. RESPECT THEIR MOM.

LAUGH OVER SPILT MILK. QUIT SMOKING.

RESPOND TO ANY CRISIS: "I LOVE YOU. IT'LL BE OKAY. WE'LL GET THROUGH THIS TOGETHER."

HOLD YOUR BABY. TUCK IN. SAY BEDTIME PRAYERS.

RAKE LEAVES TOGETHER. STOP RAKING TO WATCH THE GEESE FLY SOUTH IN "V" FORMATION.

IGNORE THE STICKBALL DENTS ON THE GARAGE DOOR.

WAKE YOUR KID FOR A LUNAR ECLIPSE.

MAKE STILTS. SUDDENLY YOUR 8-YEAR-OLD IS LOOKING YOU IN THE EYE.

QUIT GOLF. OR PATIENTLY TEACH THEM TO PLAY GOLF.

TEACH ROCK/PAPER/SCISSORS. TELL KNOCK-KNOCK JOKES. GIVE HORSEY RIDES.

PLAY H-O-R-S-E. DON'T LET THEM WIN. THEY'LL BEAT YOU FAIR AND SQUARE SOON ENOUGH.

The DAD MANIFESTO

52 THINGS FOR FOREVER FATHERS TO NEVER FORGET

KISS YOUR WIFE IN THE KITCHEN.

DON'T BE THE JERK IN THE STANDS.

CHAPERONE A SCHOOL DANCE.

EARN THE RIGHT TO SAY WHAT NEEDS TO BE SAID.

CHAT OVER WAFFLES.

STOP AT HISTORICAL MARKERS.

CUDDLE.

SKIP ROCKS. ALWAYS HAVE A CLEAN HANDKERCHIEF.

VOLUNTEER AT THEIR SCHOOL OR YOUTH GROUP.

WRITE "LOVE YOU" ON A STICKY NOTE. APOLOGIZE

KEEP PROMISES. SOMETIMES SAY NO. WHEN YOU MESS UP.

RESCUE THEM AT THE TOP OF ANY SLIPPERY SLOPE.

MAKE TIME FOR THEM. THEY'LL MAKE TIME FOR YOU LATER. CARRY RECENT PHOTOS ON YOUR SMARTPHONE.

BE AMAZED WHEN THEY BRING YOU A BUG, DANDELION, OR SHINY ROCK. MAKE YOUR HOME A HANGOUT.

CALL, TEXT, OR REACH OUT TO THEM RIGHT NOW.

BE THERE, DAD. BE AN AWESOME GRANDPA.

TEACH THEM HOW TO LOVE.

TEACH THEM HOW TO BE LOVED.

The Dad Manifesto © 2011
Words by Jay Payleitner
Author/Speaker: jaypayleitner.com
Design by Pat Sohn. patsohn.com

33

CHAT OVER WAFFLES.

These commandments that I give you today are to be on your hearts. Impress them on your children. Talk about them when you sit at home and when you walk along the road, when you lie down and when you get up.

DEUTERONOMY 6:6-7

You know things your kids need to know. You've learned lessons your kids need to learn. To pass on your wisdom, you need to do life with your kids.

Especially as they get older, intentionally orchestrate opportunities that bring you face-to-face or side by side. Working. Traveling. Playing. Golfing. Competing. Gardening. Cooking. Stargazing. Dancing. Dining. Going out for ice cream. Strolling a beach. Shopping for a Mother's Day present. Or serving dinner in a homeless shelter. You get the idea.

Dad, feel free to interpret the above passage from Deuteronomy to suggest, "Talk to your kids about stuff that matters when you're watching TV commercials, riding in the car, strolling down a dirt road, tucking them in, or munching on blueberry waffles at your favorite diner." Do life together, and chatting will occur spontaneously.

STOP AND CATCH THE FIREFLIES. LAUGH WITH THEM. CRY WITH THEM. GIVE NOOGIES. ANSWER THEIR QUESTIONS WITH QUESTIONS. DON'T CURSE THE TRAIN, COUNT THE CARS. SPY ON YOUR KIDS. BUY A UNICYCLE. SNUGGLE. RESPECT THEIR MOM. LAUGH OVER SPILT MILK. QUIT SMOKING. RESPOND TO ANY CRISIS, "I LOVE YOU. I'LL BE OKAY. WE'LL GET THROUGH THIS TOGETHER." HOLD YOUR BABY. TUCK IN. SAY BEDTIME PRAYERS. RAKE LEAVES TOGETHER. STOP RAKING TO WATCH THE GEESE FLY SOUTH IN "V" FORMATION. IGNORE THE STICKBALL DENTS ON THE GARAGE DOOR. WAKE YOUR KID FOR A LUNAR ECLIPSE. MAKE STILTS. SUDDENLY YOUR 8-YEAR-OLD IS LOOKING YOU IN THE EYE. QUIT GOLF. OR PATIENTLY TEACH THEM TO PLAY GOLF. TEACH ROCK/PAPER/SCISSORS. TELL KNOCK-KNOCK JOKES. GIVE HORSEY RIDES.

PLAY H-O-R-S-E. DON'T LET THEM WIN. THEY'LL BEAT YOU FAIR AND SQUARE SOON ENOUGH. EARN THE RIGHT TO SAY WHAT NEEDS TO BE SAID. CHAT OVER WAFFLES.

The DAD MANIFESTO
52 THINGS FOR FOREVER FATHERS TO NEVER FORGET

KISS YOUR WIFE IN THE KITCHEN. DON'T BE THE JERK IN THE STANDS. CHAPERONE A SCHOOL DANCE. CUDDLE.

STOP AT HISTORICAL MARKERS.

SKIP ROCKS. ALWAYS HAVE A CLEAN HANDKERCHIEF. VOLUNTEER AT THEIR SCHOOL OR YOUTH GROUP. WRITE "LOVE YOU" ON A STICKY NOTE. APOLOGIZE KEEP PROMISES. SOMETIMES SAY NO. WHEN YOU MESS UP. RESCUE THEM AT THE TOP OF ANY SLIPPERY SLOPE. MAKE TIME FOR THEM. THEY'LL MAKE TIME FOR YOU LATER. CARRY RECENT PHOTOS ON YOUR SMARTPHONE. BE AMAZED WHEN THEY BRING YOU A BUG, DANDELION, OR SHINY ROCK. MAKE YOUR HOME A HANGOUT. CALL, TEXT, OR REACH OUT TO THEM RIGHT NOW. BE THERE, DAD. BE AN AWESOME GRANDPA. TEACH THEM HOW TO LOVE. TEACH THEM HOW TO BE LOVED.

34

STOP AT HISTORICAL MARKERS.

Finally, brothers and sisters, whatever is true, whatever is noble, whatever is right, whatever is pure, whatever is lovely, whatever is admirable—if anything is excellent or praiseworthy—think about such things.

PHILIPPIANS 4:8

Some determined dads whiz by America on the interstate highways. They arrive sooner at the end point, but they miss the middle. Stopping at historical markers, trading posts, greasy spoons, geological landmarks, mom-and-pop stores, and even the occasional tourist trap is what makes a vacation a vacation.

Getting out of the car, stretching your legs, keeping your eyes open for the weird and the wonderful...these things give you a chance to discover or learn something you didn't know before. Doing it together as a family is how memories are made.

By the way, insist your kids put down their screens for part of the trip. Unless of course they're searching the latest travel app for the next roadside attraction.

STOP AND CATCH THE FIREFLIES. LAUGH WITH THEM. CRY WITH THEM. GIVE NOOGIES.

ANSWER THEIR QUESTIONS WITH QUESTIONS.

DON'T CURSE THE TRAIN, COUNT THE CARS.

SPY ON YOUR KIDS. BUY A UNICYCLE.

SNUGGLE. RESPECT THEIR MOM.

LAUGH OVER SPILT MILK. QUIT SMOKING.

RESPOND TO ANY CRISIS, "I LOVE YOU. IT'LL BE OKAY. WE'LL GET THROUGH THIS TOGETHER."

HOLD YOUR BABY. TUCK IN. SAY BEDTIME PRAYERS.

RAKE LEAVES TOGETHER. STOP RAKING TO WATCH THE GEESE FLY SOUTH IN A "V" FORMATION.

IGNORE THE STICKBALL DENTS ON THE GARAGE DOOR.

WAKE YOUR KID FOR A LUNAR ECLIPSE. MAKE STILTS.

SUDDENLY YOUR 8-YEAR-OLD IS LOOKING YOU IN THE EYE.

QUIT GOLF. OR PATIENTLY TEACH THEM TO PLAY GOLF.

TEACH ROCK/PAPER/SCISSORS. TELL KNOCK-KNOCK JOKES. GIVE HORSEY RIDES.

PLAY H-O-R-S-E. DON'T LET THEM WIN. THEY'LL BEAT YOU FAIR AND SQUARE SOON ENOUGH.

KISS YOUR WIFE IN THE KITCHEN.

DON'T BE THE JERK IN THE STANDS.

EARN THE RIGHT TO SAY WHAT NEEDS TO BE SAID.

CHAPERONE A SCHOOL DANCE.

CHAT OVER WAFFLES.

STOP AT HISTORICAL MARKERS.

CUDDLE.

SKIP ROCKS. ALWAYS HAVE A CLEAN HANDKERCHIEF.

VOLUNTEER AT THEIR SCHOOL OR YOUTH GROUP.

WRITE "LOVE YOU" ON A STICKY NOTE. APOLOGIZE

KEEP PROMISES. SOMETIMES SAY NO. WHEN YOU MESS UP.

RESCUE THEM AT THE TOP OF ANY SLIPPERY SLOPE.

MAKE TIME FOR THEM. THEY'LL MAKE TIME FOR YOU LATER. CARRY RECENT PHOTOS ON YOUR SMARTPHONE.

BE AMAZED WHEN THEY BRING YOU A BUG, DANDELION, OR SHINY ROCK. MAKE YOUR HOME A HANGOUT. CALL, TEXT, OR REACH OUT TO THEM RIGHT NOW.

BE THERE, DAD. BE AN AWESOME GRANDPA.

TEACH THEM HOW TO LOVE.

TEACH THEM HOW TO BE LOVED.

The Dad Manifesto
52 THINGS FOR FOREVER FATHERS TO NEVER FORGET

35

CUDDLE.

Love never fails.

1 CORINTHIANS 13:8

Not to be confused with the activity of snuggling, cuddling is an end goal. It's a momentary or prolonged surrender to the warmth, love, and devotion of family. In most cases, the only thought process occurring during a good cuddle is appreciation of the cuddle. It's a physical manifestation of love.

Never force a cuddle, but let's pledge to increase family cuddle time. A dad lies on the couch with his newborn sleeping on his chest. A girl sits in her daddy's lap. A dad curls up on the bedspread next to a youngster who just had a bad dream. Looking up at the clouds, a kid and dad share the same patch of grass. A prolonged standing hug could even be considered a cuddle. I have no research on this, but I believe cuddling begets more cuddling.

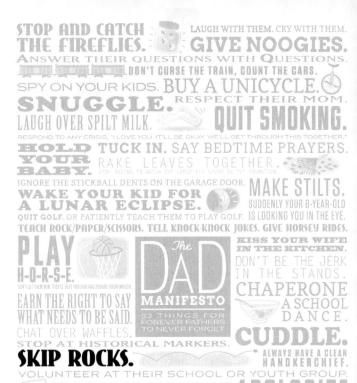

STOP AND CATCH THE FIREFLIES.
LAUGH WITH THEM. CRY WITH THEM.
GIVE NOOGIES.
ANSWER THEIR QUESTIONS WITH QUESTIONS.
DON'T CURSE THE TRAIN, COUNT THE CARS.
SPY ON YOUR KIDS. BUY A UNICYCLE.
SNUGGLE. RESPECT THEIR MOM.
LAUGH OVER SPILT MILK. QUIT SMOKING.
RESPOND TO ANY CRISIS, "I LOVE YOU. IT'LL BE OKAY. WE'LL GET THROUGH THIS TOGETHER."
HOLD YOUR BABY. TUCK IN. SAY BEDTIME PRAYERS.
RAKE LEAVES TOGETHER.
STOP TRYING TO WATCH THE GEESE FLY SOUTH IN "V" FORMATION.
IGNORE THE STICKBALL DENTS ON THE GARAGE DOOR.
WAKE YOUR KID FOR A LUNAR ECLIPSE. MAKE STILTS.
QUIT GOLF. OR PATIENTLY TEACH THEM TO PLAY GOLF. SUDDENLY YOUR 8-YEAR-OLD IS LOOKING YOU IN THE EYE.
TEACH ROCK/PAPER/SCISSORS. TELL KNOCK-KNOCK JOKES. GIVE HORSEY RIDES.
PLAY H-O-R-S-E.
DON'T LET THEM WIN. THEY'LL BEAT YOU FAIR AND SQUARE SOON ENOUGH.
KISS YOUR WIFE IN THE KITCHEN.
DON'T BE THE JERK IN THE STANDS.
CHAPERONE A SCHOOL DANCE.
The DAD MANIFESTO
52 THINGS FOR FOREVER FATHERS TO NEVER FORGET
EARN THE RIGHT TO SAY WHAT NEEDS TO BE SAID.
CHAT OVER WAFFLES.
STOP AT HISTORICAL MARKERS.
CUDDLE.
SKIP ROCKS. ALWAYS HAVE A CLEAN HANDKERCHIEF.
VOLUNTEER AT THEIR SCHOOL OR YOUTH GROUP.
Love you WRITE "LOVE YOU" ON A STICKY NOTE. APOLOGIZE
KEEP PROMISES. SOMETIMES SAY NO. WHEN YOU MESS UP.
RESCUE THEM AT THE TOP OF ANY SLIPPERY SLOPE.
MAKE TIME FOR THEM. CARRY RECENT PHOTOS
THEY'LL MAKE TIME FOR YOU LATER. ON YOUR SMARTPHONE.
BE AMAZED MAKE YOUR HOME A HANGOUT.
WHEN THEY BRING YOU A BUG, CALL, TEXT, OR REACH OUT
DANDELION, OR SHINY ROCK. TO THEM RIGHT NOW.
BE THERE, DAD. BE AN AWESOME GRANDPA.
TEACH THEM HOW TO LOVE.
TEACH THEM HOW TO BE LOVED.

The Dad Manifesto © 2014
Words by Jay Payleitner,
author/speaker, JayPayleitner.com
Design by Rex John, rexjohn.com

36

SKIP ROCKS.

And whatever you do, whether in word or deed,
do it all in the name of the Lord Jesus, giving
thanks to God the Father through him.

COLOSSIANS 3:17

Did your dad teach you this critical life skill? Remember choosing just the right stone? Flat, but not too thin. Just the right circumference so that it fits comfortably in your fingers. With just enough weight that it skips and doesn't plop into the water. Then learning how to lean low and aim parallel to the surface of the pond or creek. Letting it fly. Part throw, part flip.

Three skips was a good start. But soon anything less than five skips was a fail. It took some practice but not hours. When a dad skips rocks with his child, he uses every teaching skill in the book. Words. Touch. Choice. Demonstration. Correction. Patience. Practice. Competition. Cheers.

By the way. This all takes place outside. Dads and kids today need more time outside.

STOP AND CATCH THE FIREFLIES.
LAUGH WITH THEM. CRY WITH THEM.
GIVE NOOGIES.
ANSWER THEIR QUESTIONS WITH QUESTIONS.
DON'T CURSE THE TRAIN, COUNT THE CARS.
SPY ON YOUR KIDS. BUY A UNICYCLE.
SNUGGLE. RESPECT THEIR MOM.
LAUGH OVER SPILT MILK. QUIT SMOKING.
RESPOND TO ANY CRISIS, "I LOVE YOU. IT'LL BE OKAY. WE'LL GET THROUGH THIS TOGETHER."
HOLD YOUR BABY. TUCK IN. SAY BEDTIME PRAYERS.
RAKE LEAVES TOGETHER.
STOP RAKING TO WATCH THE BEST FLY SOUTH IN "V" FORMATION.
IGNORE THE STICKBALL DENTS ON THE GARAGE DOOR.
WAKE YOUR KID FOR A LUNAR ECLIPSE.
MAKE STILTS.
SUDDENLY YOUR 8-YEAR-OLD
QUIT GOLF. OR PATIENTLY TEACH THEM TO PLAY GOLF. IS LOOKING YOU IN THE EYE.
TEACH ROCK/PAPER/SCISSORS. TELL KNOCK-KNOCK JOKES. GIVE HORSEY RIDES.

PLAY H-O-R-S-E.
DON'T LET THEM WIN. THEY'LL BEAT YOU FAIR AND SQUARE SOON ENOUGH.
EARN THE RIGHT TO SAY WHAT NEEDS TO BE SAID.
CHAT OVER WAFFLES.
STOP AT HISTORICAL MARKERS.
SKIP ROCKS.

The DAD MANIFESTO
52 THINGS FOR FOREVER FATHERS TO NEVER FORGET

KISS YOUR WIFE IN THE KITCHEN.
DON'T BE THE JERK IN THE STANDS.
CHAPERONE A SCHOOL DANCE.
CUDDLE.
ALWAYS HAVE A CLEAN HANDKERCHIEF.

VOLUNTEER AT THEIR SCHOOL OR YOUTH GROUP.
WRITE "LOVE YOU" ON A STICKY NOTE. APOLOGIZE
KEEP PROMISES. SOMETIMES SAY NO. WHEN YOU MESS UP.
RESCUE THEM AT THE TOP OF ANY SLIPPERY SLOPE.
MAKE TIME FOR THEM. CARRY RECENT PHOTOS
THEY'LL MAKE TIME FOR YOU LATER. ON YOUR SMARTPHONE.
BE AMAZED MAKE YOUR HOME A HANGOUT.
WHEN THEY BRING YOU A BUG, CALL, TEXT, OR REACH OUT
DANDELION, OR SHINY ROCK. TO THEM RIGHT NOW.
BE THERE, DAD. BE AN AWESOME GRANDPA.
TEACH THEM HOW TO LOVE.
TEACH THEM HOW TO BE LOVED.

37

ALWAYS HAVE A CLEAN HANDKERCHIEF.

*Praise be to the God and Father of our Lord Jesus
Christ, the Father of compassion and the God of
all comfort, who comforts us in all our troubles,
so that we can comfort those in any trouble with
the comfort we ourselves receive from God.*

2 CORINTHIANS 1:3-4

Mom's purse should always have hand sanitizer, nail clippers, matches, breath mints, Band-Aids, tissues, pen, paper, and something to help a headache. Dad should always carry a clean hankie.

Perhaps it's a throwback to the days when a gallant man offered his handkerchief to a lady weeping at a wedding or funeral while the man stands by stoically. They also come in handy for a myriad of other manly reasons. As a tourniquet to stop severe bleeding. To clean spectacles. To dry your hands when today's loud, air-blowing hand dryers fail. To mop your brow after performing manly duties in the sun. To blow your nose. And, if absolutely necessary, to signal surrender to an enemy.

Maybe carry two. Handkerchief etiquette suggests you never ask for it back, even if it's monogrammed.

38

VOLUNTEER AT THEIR SCHOOL OR YOUTH GROUP.

*One generation commends your works to
another; they tell of your mighty acts.*

PSALM 145:4

Here's a great hint for dads. Do what moms do. For generations, moms have been showing up at elementary schools to help at holiday classroom parties, chaperone field trips to local museums, and serve as lunchroom helpers and playground monitors. Well, step up, Dad!

It's no longer unimaginable for dads to volunteer at an elementary school, but kids still react with delight when a dad walks in a classroom or strolls the playground. The national organization WATCH D.O.G.S. (Dads of Great Students) even has a program for men to sign up to spend one day each school year at their child's school. You can be the hero of the hallway.

Church youth pastors are always looking for adult volunteers. Keep your eyes open, and you'll encounter plenty of young people who could use your wise, fatherly insight.

STOP AND CATCH THE FIREFLIES. LAUGH WITH THEM. CRY WITH THEM. GIVE NOOGIES. ANSWER THEIR QUESTIONS WITH QUESTIONS. DON'T CURSE THE TRAIN, COUNT THE CARS. SPY ON YOUR KIDS. BUY A UNICYCLE. SNUGGLE. RESPECT THEIR MOM. LAUGH OVER SPILT MILK. QUIT SMOKING. RESPOND TO ANY CRISIS, "I LOVE YOU. IT'LL BE OKAY. WE'LL GET THROUGH THIS TOGETHER." HOLD YOUR BABY. TUCK IN. SAY BEDTIME PRAYERS. RAKE LEAVES TOGETHER. STOP RAKING TO WATCH THE GEESE FLY SOUTH IN 'V' FORMATION. IGNORE THE STICKBALL DENTS ON THE GARAGE DOOR. WAKE YOUR KID FOR A LUNAR ECLIPSE. MAKE STILTS. SUDDENLY YOUR 8-YEAR-OLD IS LOOKING YOU IN THE EYE. QUIT GOLF. OR PATIENTLY TEACH THEM TO PLAY GOLF. TEACH ROCK/PAPER/SCISSORS. TELL KNOCK-KNOCK JOKES. GIVE HORSEY RIDES.

PLAY H-O-R-S-E. DON'T LET THEM WIN. THEY'LL BEAT YOU FAIR AND SQUARE SOON ENOUGH. EARN THE RIGHT TO SAY WHAT NEEDS TO BE SAID. CHAT OVER WAFFLES. STOP AT HISTORICAL MARKERS. SKIP ROCKS.

The DAD MANIFESTO
52 THINGS FOR FOREVER FATHERS TO NEVER FORGET

KISS YOUR WIFE IN THE KITCHEN. DON'T BE THE JERK IN THE STANDS. CHAPERONE A SCHOOL DANCE. CUDDLE. ALWAYS HAVE A CLEAN HANDKERCHIEF.

VOLUNTEER AT THEIR SCHOOL OR YOUTH GROUP. WRITE "LOVE YOU" ON A STICKY NOTE. APOLOGIZE KEEP PROMISES. SOMETIMES SAY NO. WHEN YOU MESS UP. RESCUE THEM AT THE TOP OF ANY SLIPPERY SLOPE. MAKE TIME FOR THEM. THEY'LL MAKE TIME FOR YOU LATER. CARRY RECENT PHOTOS ON YOUR SMARTPHONE. BE AMAZED WHEN THEY BRING YOU A BUG, DANDELION, OR SHINY ROCK. MAKE YOUR HOME A HANGOUT. CALL, TEXT, OR REACH OUT TO THEM RIGHT NOW. BE THERE, DAD. BE AN AWESOME GRANDPA. TEACH THEM HOW TO LOVE. TEACH THEM HOW TO BE LOVED.

The Dad Manifesto © 2014
Words by Jay Payleitner.
Author/Speaker, jaypayleitner.com
Design by Koy Flink, rockfnd.com

39

WRITE "LOVE YOU" ON A STICKY NOTE.

*A word fitly spoken is like apples
of gold in settings of silver.*
PROVERBS 25:11 NKJV

Even a quiet dad can deliver short, encouraging phrases to his kids on a regular basis. "Nice job." "Proud of you." "Well done." "Well played." "XXXO, Dad" "Be epic today!" "Good luck at tryouts." "Break a leg!" "Thanks for being you." "Love you."

Vocalize these ideas as your kids head out the door. Whisper them as you kiss their forehead after bedtime prayers. Jot them on yellow Post-it notes and stick them on their mirror, desktop, lunch box, book bag, or steering wheel. Notes are especially valuable when busy dads and busy kids seem to be racing past each other for days in a row.

Don't be surprised if they keep them stuck where you stick them—or collect them! Your kids will appreciate each thoughtful message over and over for weeks to come.

STOP AND CATCH THE FIREFLIES. LAUGH WITH THEM. CRY WITH THEM. GIVE NOOGIES.

ANSWER THEIR QUESTIONS WITH QUESTIONS.

DON'T CURSE THE TRAIN, COUNT THE CARS.

SPY ON YOUR KIDS. BUY A UNICYCLE.

SNUGGLE. RESPECT THEIR MOM.

LAUGH OVER SPILT MILK. QUIT SMOKING.

RESPOND TO ANY CRISIS, "I LOVE YOU. IT'LL BE OKAY. WE'LL GET THROUGH THIS TOGETHER."

HOLD YOUR BABY. TUCK IN. SAY BEDTIME PRAYERS. RAKE LEAVES TOGETHER. STOP RAKING TO WATCH THE GEESE FLY SOUTH IN "V" FORMATION.

IGNORE THE STICKBALL DENTS ON THE GARAGE DOOR.

WAKE YOUR KID FOR A LUNAR ECLIPSE. MAKE STILTS. SUDDENLY YOUR 8-YEAR-OLD IS LOOKING YOU IN THE EYE.

QUIT GOLF. OR PATIENTLY TEACH THEM TO PLAY GOLF.

TEACH ROCK/PAPER/SCISSORS. TELL KNOCK-KNOCK JOKES. GIVE HORSEY RIDES.

PLAY H-O-R-S-E. DON'T LET THEM WIN. THEY'LL BEAT YOU FAIR AND SQUARE SOON ENOUGH.

The DAD MANIFESTO 52 THINGS FOR FOREVER FATHERS TO NEVER FORGET

KISS YOUR WIFE IN THE KITCHEN. DON'T BE THE JERK IN THE STANDS. CHAPERONE A SCHOOL DANCE.

EARN THE RIGHT TO SAY WHAT NEEDS TO BE SAID. CHAT OVER WAFFLES.

STOP AT HISTORICAL MARKERS. CUDDLE.

SKIP ROCKS. ALWAYS HAVE A CLEAN HANDKERCHIEF.

VOLUNTEER AT THEIR SCHOOL OR YOUTH GROUP.

WRITE "LOVE YOU" ON A STICKY NOTE. APOLOGIZE WHEN YOU MESS UP.

KEEP PROMISES. SOMETIMES SAY NO.

RESCUE THEM AT THE TOP OF ANY SLIPPERY SLOPE.

MAKE TIME FOR THEM. THEY'LL MAKE TIME FOR YOU LATER. CARRY RECENT PHOTOS ON YOUR SMARTPHONE.

BE AMAZED WHEN THEY BRING YOU A BUG, DANDELION, OR SHINY ROCK. MAKE YOUR HOME A HANGOUT. CALL, TEXT, OR REACH OUT TO THEM RIGHT NOW.

BE THERE, DAD. BE AN AWESOME GRANDPA.

TEACH THEM HOW TO LOVE. TEACH THEM HOW TO BE LOVED.

40

APOLOGIZE
WHEN YOU MESS UP.

*Make allowance for each other's faults, and
forgive anyone who offends you. Remember, the
Lord forgave you, so you must forgive others.
Above all, clothe yourselves with love, which
binds us all together in perfect harmony.*

COLOSSIANS 3:13-14 NLT

Dads need to be good at apologizing. That's because we mess up more often than kids and moms put together.

Kids are still figuring life out, so really we can't fault them too much when they make mistakes. Trial and error is an important skill for kids.

Moms, of course, are not risk takers like dads. Men of action—like you and me—forge ahead and speak our minds even when we haven't thought about all the possible consequences.

Take it from someone who errs frequently and apologizes often. When you mess up—and you will—ask for forgiveness without delay. Give your family the opportunity to extend grace. If you delay, deny, or blame others, what are you teaching your kids?

STOP AND CATCH THE FIREFLIES. LAUGH WITH THEM. CRY WITH THEM. GIVE NOOGIES. ANSWER THEIR QUESTIONS WITH QUESTIONS. DON'T CURSE THE TRAIN, COUNT THE CARS. SPY ON YOUR KIDS. BUY A UNICYCLE. SNUGGLE. RESPECT THEIR MOM. LAUGH OVER SPILT MILK. QUIT SMOKING. RESPOND TO ANY CRISIS, "I LOVE YOU. IT'LL BE OKAY. WE'LL GET THROUGH THIS TOGETHER." HOLD YOUR BABY. TUCK IN. SAY BEDTIME PRAYERS. RAKE LEAVES TOGETHER. STOP RAKING TO WATCH THE GEESE FLY SOUTH IN "V" FORMATION. IGNORE THE STICKBALL DENTS ON THE GARAGE DOOR. MAKE STILTS. WAKE YOUR KID FOR A LUNAR ECLIPSE. SUDDENLY YOUR 8-YEAR-OLD IS LOOKING YOU IN THE EYE. QUIT GOLF. OR PATIENTLY TEACH THEM TO PLAY GOLF. TEACH ROCK/PAPER/SCISSORS. TELL KNOCK-KNOCK JOKES. GIVE HORSEY RIDES. PLAY H-O-R-S-E. DON'T LET THEM WIN. THEY'LL BEAT YOU FAIR AND SQUARE SOON ENOUGH. EARN THE RIGHT TO SAY WHAT NEEDS TO BE SAID. CHAT OVER WAFFLES. STOP AT HISTORICAL MARKERS. SKIP ROCKS. KISS YOUR WIFE IN THE KITCHEN. DON'T BE THE JERK IN THE STANDS. CHAPERONE A SCHOOL DANCE. CUDDLE. ALWAYS HAVE A CLEAN HANDKERCHIEF. VOLUNTEER AT THEIR SCHOOL OR YOUTH GROUP. WRITE "LOVE YOU" ON A STICKY NOTE. APOLOGIZE WHEN YOU MESS UP. KEEP PROMISES. SOMETIMES SAY NO. RESCUE THEM AT THE TOP OF ANY SLIPPERY SLOPE. MAKE TIME FOR THEM. THEY'LL MAKE TIME FOR YOU LATER. CARRY RECENT PHOTOS ON YOUR SMARTPHONE. BE AMAZED WHEN THEY BRING YOU A BUG, DANDELION, OR SHINY ROCK. MAKE YOUR HOME A HANGOUT. CALL, TEXT, OR REACH OUT TO THEM RIGHT NOW. BE THERE, DAD. BE AN AWESOME GRANDPA. TEACH THEM HOW TO LOVE. TEACH THEM HOW TO BE LOVED.

The DAD MANIFESTO
52 THINGS FOR FOREVER FATHERS TO NEVER FORGET

41

KEEP PROMISES.

*Honor your father and mother. Then
you will live a long, full life in the land
the LORD your God is giving you.*

EXODUS 20:12 NLT

My dad had a clever stalling tactic that worked well—for a while. Whenever we kids asked to do something or go somewhere, he would say, "We'll see." That may sound like a brilliant fathering strategy. Except we all caught on and figured out he was really just saying no.

As a dad, I pledged to never say, "We'll see." Which meant that often I would say, "Sure, we can do that." And then, sometimes, we didn't. After about four or five broken promises, I learned to make only those promises I could and would keep. I haven't broken one since.

By the way, the fifth commandment is the only commandment that comes with a promise. Share it with your kids. Some nonbiblical scholars interpret that verse, "Be excellent to your folks and get real estate."

42

SOMETIMES SAY **NO.**

He must increase, but I must decrease.
JOHN 3:30 NASB

Remember this story? Jesus had come to visit two sisters, and Martha was ticked that she was doing all the work. Martha asked Jesus to insist her sister help in the kitchen. Jesus said no and affirmed, "Mary has chosen what is better" (Luke 10:38-42).

How about this story? A would-be follower asks for a few days to say good-bye to his family. Jesus said no and confirmed that once you choose him, there's no turning back (Luke 9:61-62).

Here's the deal on saying no to your kids. It's good practice for them. They need to know they can't always get what they want here on earth. They might even have a legitimate and worthy request. But in life, sometimes even reasonable proposals are overruled. Always say yes to God. Sometimes say no to yourself.

43

RESCUE THEM AT THE TOP OF ANY SLIPPERY SLOPE.

But those who won't care for their relatives, especially those in their own household, have denied the true faith. Such people are worse than unbelievers.

1 TIMOTHY 5:8 NLT

Kids make mistakes. That's actually a good thing. That's how they learn. Often your best choice is to let natural consequences take their course. If you step in, they stop learning.

But sometimes the risk is too risky. That's when a dad needs to find the courage to do whatever it takes to rescue his wayward child.

Here's a guiding principle. A father needs to intervene if the aftermath is life threatening, permanently damaging to their reputation and witness, or likely robbing them of a major opportunity in the near future.

Know your child. Understand that some slopes—things like drugs, alcohol, violent behavior, vandalism, sexual promiscuity, and gang involvement—are terrifyingly slippery. Know that your child is counting on you to be their hero. Whether they say it or not.

STOP AND CATCH THE FIREFLIES. LAUGH WITH THEM. CRY WITH THEM. GIVE NOOGIES.

ANSWER THEIR QUESTIONS WITH QUESTIONS.

DON'T CURSE THE TRAIN, COUNT THE CARS.

SPY ON YOUR KIDS. BUY A UNICYCLE.

SNUGGLE. RESPECT THEIR MOM.

LAUGH OVER SPILT MILK. QUIT SMOKING.

RESPOND TO ANY CRISIS, "I LOVE YOU. IT'LL BE OKAY. WE'LL GET THROUGH THIS TOGETHER."

HOLD YOUR BABY. TUCK IN. SAY BEDTIME PRAYERS.

RAKE LEAVES TOGETHER.
STOP RAKING TO WATCH THE GEESE FLY SOUTH IN "V" FORMATION.

IGNORE THE STICKBALL DENTS ON THE GARAGE DOOR.

WAKE YOUR KID FOR A LUNAR ECLIPSE. MAKE STILTS.

SUDDENLY YOUR 8-YEAR-OLD

QUIT GOLF. OR PATIENTLY TEACH THEM TO PLAY GOLF. IS LOOKING YOU IN THE EYE.

TEACH ROCK/PAPER/SCISSORS. TELL KNOCK-KNOCK JOKES. GIVE HORSEY RIDES.

PLAY H-O-R-S-E.
DON'T LET THEM WIN. THEY'LL BEAT YOU FAIR AND SQUARE SOON ENOUGH.

KISS YOUR WIFE IN THE KITCHEN.

DON'T BE THE JERK IN THE STANDS.

EARN THE RIGHT TO SAY WHAT NEEDS TO BE SAID.

CHAPERONE A SCHOOL DANCE.

The DAD MANIFESTO
52 THINGS FOR FOREVER FATHERS TO NEVER FORGET

CHAT OVER WAFFLES.

STOP AT HISTORICAL MARKERS. CUDDLE.

SKIP ROCKS.

ALWAYS HAVE A CLEAN HANDKERCHIEF.

VOLUNTEER AT THEIR SCHOOL OR YOUTH GROUP.

WRITE "LOVE YOU" ON A STICKY NOTE. APOLOGIZE

KEEP PROMISES. SOMETIMES SAY NO. WHEN YOU MESS UP.

RESCUE THEM AT THE TOP OF ANY SLIPPERY SLOPE.

MAKE TIME FOR THEM. THEY'LL MAKE TIME FOR YOU LATER.

CARRY RECENT PHOTOS ON YOUR SMARTPHONE.

BE AMAZED
WHEN THEY BRING YOU A BUG, DANDELION, OR SHINY ROCK.

MAKE YOUR HOME A HANGOUT.

CALL, TEXT, OR REACH OUT TO THEM RIGHT NOW.

BE THERE, DAD. BE AN AWESOME GRANDPA.

TEACH THEM HOW TO LOVE.

TEACH THEM HOW TO BE LOVED.

MAKE TIME FOR THEM.
THEY'LL MAKE TIME FOR YOU LATER.

*When I was a child, I spoke and thought
and reasoned as a child. But when I
grew up, I put away childish things.*
1 CORINTHIANS 13:11 NLT

Author and speaker Josh McDowell recalls the afternoon, decades ago, when his young son came into his office. Sean asked innocently, "Want to play, Dad?" Like so many fathers, Josh responded, "Son, Daddy's busy. How about a little later?"

Young Sean trotted off without complaining. A moment later, Josh's wife, Dottie, came in and shared some memorable words of wisdom. "Honey, you will always have a deadline to meet, a talk to prepare, and a trip somewhere to give it. But, honey, you won't always have a two-year-old son who wants to sit in his daddy's lap and show you his new ball."

She started to walk out but stopped to make one final point. "You know, if you spend time with your kids now, they'll spend time with you later."

STOP AND CATCH THE FIREFLIES.  LAUGH WITH THEM. CRY WITH THEM. GIVE NOOGIES.

ANSWER THEIR QUESTIONS WITH QUESTIONS. DON'T CURSE THE TRAIN, COUNT THE CARS.

SPY ON YOUR KIDS. BUY A UNICYCLE.

SNUGGLE. RESPECT THEIR MOM.

LAUGH OVER SPILT MILK. QUIT SMOKING.

RESPOND TO ANY CRISIS. "I LOVE YOU. IT'LL BE OKAY. WE'LL GET THROUGH THIS TOGETHER."

HOLD YOUR BABY. TUCK IN. SAY BEDTIME PRAYERS.

RAKE LEAVES TOGETHER. STOP RAKING IN RADISH THE LEAVES FLY SOUTH IN "V" FORMATION.

IGNORE THE STICKBALL DENTS ON THE GARAGE DOOR.

WAKE YOUR KID FOR A LUNAR ECLIPSE. MAKE STILTS. SUDDENLY YOUR 8-YEAR-OLD IS LOOKING YOU IN THE EYE.

QUIT GOLF. OR PATIENTLY TEACH THEM TO PLAY GOLF.

TEACH ROCK/PAPER/SCISSORS. TELL KNOCK-KNOCK JOKES. GIVE HORSEY RIDES.

PLAY H-O-R-S-E. DON'T LET THEM WIN. THEY'LL BEAT YOU FAIR AND SQUARE SOON ENOUGH.

KISS YOUR WIFE IN THE KITCHEN. DON'T BE THE JERK IN THE STANDS.

CHAPERONE A SCHOOL DANCE.

EARN THE RIGHT TO SAY WHAT NEEDS TO BE SAID. CHAT OVER WAFFLES.

STOP AT HISTORICAL MARKERS. CUDDLE.

The DAD MANIFESTO 52 THINGS FOR FOREVER FATHERS TO NEVER FORGET

SKIP ROCKS. ALWAYS HAVE A CLEAN HANDKERCHIEF.

VOLUNTEER AT THEIR SCHOOL OR YOUTH GROUP.

WRITE "LOVE YOU" ON A STICKY NOTE. APOLOGIZE WHEN YOU MESS UP.

KEEP PROMISES. SOMETIMES SAY NO.

RESCUE THEM AT THE TOP OF ANY SLIPPERY SLOPE.

MAKE TIME FOR THEM. THEY'LL MAKE TIME FOR YOU LATER. CARRY RECENT PHOTOS ON YOUR SMARTPHONE.

BE AMAZED WHEN THEY BRING YOU A BUG, DANDELION, OR SHINY ROCK. MAKE YOUR HOME A HANGOUT. CALL, TEXT, OR REACH OUT TO THEM RIGHT NOW.

BE THERE, DAD. BE AN AWESOME GRANDPA.

TEACH THEM HOW TO LOVE. TEACH THEM HOW TO BE LOVED.

The Dad Manifesto © 2014 Words by Jay Payleitner, Authorspeaker, jaypayleitner.com Design by Ron Kaye, rackaye.com

CARRY RECENT PHOTOS ON YOUR SMARTPHONE.

He will turn the hearts of the parents to their children, and the hearts of the children to their parents; or else I will come and strike the land with total destruction.

MALACHI 4:6

When a dad carries photos of his family, three things happen.

One, you think about your children more. Every time you look at your phone, you're holding a piece of your family, a piece of your heart.

Two, your kids feel the connection. They know what's on your phone. They groan because they hate the way they look in that picture, but they're glad you're carrying it.

Three, it's a hedge of protection for your marriage. Every time you share pics of your family, you are telling the world you place a high value on those relationships. You're off-limits to flirting. You're working to support a cause greater than yourself. You're going straight home after work. On road trips, your expense account might even reflect your more sensible lifestyle.

Dad, take your kids everywhere you go.

BE AMAZED
WHEN THEY BRING YOU A BUG, DANDELION, OR SHINY ROCK.

Children are a gift from the LORD;
they are a reward from him.
PSALM 127:3 NLT

When was the last time you made an exciting new discovery? Well, your kids are learning something wondrous and new every day. A child's natural curiosity will continue for years until someone or something compels them to stop. Don't be that killjoy.

For sure, just about everything your little one encounters will be stuff you take for granted. But, Dad, if you minimize, mock, or ignore their silly, not-so-impressive discoveries, they will probably stop making them. And that would be a terrible shame.

Instead, get down on their level. See the world through their eyes. Join their backyard expeditions and attic explorations. Be amazed. And you just might make your own new discoveries—about your kids and about yourself.

STOP AND CATCH THE FIREFLIES.  LAUGH WITH THEM. CRY WITH THEM. GIVE NOOGIES.

ANSWER THEIR QUESTIONS WITH QUESTIONS.

DON'T CURSE THE TRAIN, COUNT THE CARS.

SPY ON YOUR KIDS. BUY A UNICYCLE.

SNUGGLE. RESPECT THEIR MOM.

LAUGH OVER SPILT MILK. QUIT SMOKING.

RESPOND TO ANY CRISIS, "I LOVE YOU. IT'LL BE OKAY. WE'LL GET THROUGH THIS TOGETHER."

HOLD YOUR BABY. TUCK IN. SAY BEDTIME PRAYERS.

RAKE LEAVES TOGETHER. STOP RAKING TO WATCH THE GEESE FLY SOUTH IN "V" FORMATION.

IGNORE THE STICKBALL DENTS ON THE GARAGE DOOR.

WAKE YOUR KID FOR A LUNAR ECLIPSE. MAKE STILTS. SUDDENLY YOUR 8-YEAR-OLD IS LOOKING YOU IN THE EYE.

QUIT GOLF. OR PATIENTLY TEACH THEM TO PLAY GOLF.

TEACH ROCK/PAPER/SCISSORS. TELL KNOCK-KNOCK JOKES. GIVE HORSEY RIDES.

PLAY H-O-R-S-E. DON'T LET THEM WIN. THEY'LL BEAT YOU FAIR AND SQUARE SOON ENOUGH.

KISS YOUR WIFE IN THE KITCHEN. DON'T BE THE JERK IN THE STANDS.

CHAPERONE A SCHOOL DANCE.

EARN THE RIGHT TO SAY WHAT NEEDS TO BE SAID.

CHAT OVER WAFFLES.

STOP AT HISTORICAL MARKERS.

CUDDLE.

SKIP ROCKS. ALWAYS HAVE A CLEAN HANDKERCHIEF.

The DAD MANIFESTO
52 THINGS FOR FOREVER FATHERS TO NEVER FORGET

VOLUNTEER AT THEIR SCHOOL OR YOUTH GROUP.

WRITE "LOVE YOU" ON A STICKY NOTE. APOLOGIZE WHEN YOU MESS UP.

KEEP PROMISES. SOMETIMES SAY NO.

RESCUE THEM AT THE TOP OF ANY SLIPPERY SLOPE.

MAKE TIME FOR THEM. THEY'LL MAKE TIME FOR YOU LATER. CARRY RECENT PHOTOS ON YOUR SMARTPHONE.

BE AMAZED WHEN THEY BRING YOU A BUG, DANDELION, OR SHINY ROCK.

MAKE YOUR HOME A HANGOUT.

CALL, TEXT, OR REACH OUT TO THEM RIGHT NOW.

BE THERE, DAD. BE AN AWESOME GRANDPA.

TEACH THEM HOW TO LOVE. TEACH THEM HOW TO BE LOVED.

The Dad Manifesto © 2014
Written by Jay Payleitner
Author/speaker jaypayleitner.com
Design by Ben Kohl, ReadyOne.com

47

MAKE YOUR HOME A HANGOUT.

Let the little children come to me.
LUKE 18:16

Put a Ping-Pong table in the basement. Get ESPN. Get the latest Xbox or PlayStation karaoke game. Build a fire pit in your backyard. Stockpile junk food. When a crew of always-hungry teenagers comes over to do a group project or hang out after a game, order a couple pizzas.

What's the purpose of all this? You want to know your kids' friends. You want their friends to know you. You want *your* world to intersect with *their* world.

Establish a comfort zone in your home where kids can talk, laugh, share secrets, and make lifelong connections. On occasion, you may overhear some valuable inside scoop.

Finally, don't feel bad if your teenager has friends over to play a game or watch a movie without you. The kids are at your house, and that's a good thing!

STOP AND CATCH THE FIREFLIES. LAUGH WITH THEM. CRY WITH THEM. GIVE NOOGIES.

ANSWER THEIR QUESTIONS WITH QUESTIONS. DON'T CURSE THE TRAIN, COUNT THE CARS.

SPY ON YOUR KIDS. BUY A UNICYCLE.

SNUGGLE. RESPECT THEIR MOM.

LAUGH OVER SPILT MILK. QUIT SMOKING.

RESPOND TO ANY CRISIS, "I LOVE YOU. IT'LL BE OKAY. WE'LL GET THROUGH THIS TOGETHER."

HOLD YOUR BABY. TUCK IN. SAY BEDTIME PRAYERS.

RAKE LEAVES TOGETHER. STOP RAKING TO WATCH THE GEESE FLY SOUTH IN "V" FORMATION.

IGNORE THE STICKBALL DENTS ON THE GARAGE DOOR.

WAKE YOUR KID FOR A LUNAR ECLIPSE. MAKE STILTS. SUDDENLY YOUR 8-YEAR-OLD IS LOOKING YOU IN THE EYE.

QUIT GOLF. OR PATIENTLY TEACH THEM TO PLAY GOLF.

TEACH ROCK/PAPER/SCISSORS. TELL KNOCK-KNOCK JOKES. GIVE HORSEY RIDES.

PLAY H-O-R-S-E. DON'T LET THEM WIN. THEY'LL BEAT YOU FAIR AND SQUARE SOON ENOUGH.

KISS YOUR WIFE IN THE KITCHEN. DON'T BE THE JERK IN THE STANDS.

The Dad MANIFESTO 52 THINGS FOR FOREVER FATHERS TO NEVER FORGET

CHAPERONE A SCHOOL DANCE.

EARN THE RIGHT TO SAY WHAT NEEDS TO BE SAID.

CHAT OVER WAFFLES.

STOP AT HISTORICAL MARKERS.

CUDDLE.

SKIP ROCKS. ALWAYS HAVE A CLEAN HANDKERCHIEF.

VOLUNTEER AT THEIR SCHOOL OR YOUTH GROUP.

WRITE "LOVE YOU" ON A STICKY NOTE. APOLOGIZE

KEEP PROMISES. SOMETIMES SAY NO. WHEN YOU MESS UP.

RESCUE THEM AT THE TOP OF ANY SLIPPERY SLOPE.

MAKE TIME FOR THEM. THEY'LL MAKE TIME FOR YOU LATER. CARRY RECENT PHOTOS ON YOUR SMARTPHONE.

BE AMAZED WHEN THEY BRING YOU A BUG, DANDELION, OR SHINY ROCK. MAKE YOUR HOME A HANGOUT.

CALL, TEXT, OR REACH OUT TO THEM RIGHT NOW.

BE THERE, DAD. BE AN AWESOME GRANDPA.

TEACH THEM HOW TO LOVE.

TEACH THEM HOW TO BE LOVED.

The Dad Manifesto © 2014 Words by Jay Payleitner authorofspaces.jaypayleitner.com Design by Bob Bunn, roxbybn.com

48

CALL, TEXT, OR REACH OUT TO THEM RIGHT NOW.

Which of you, if your son asks for bread, will give him a stone? Or if he asks for a fish, will give him a snake? If you, then, though you are evil, know how to give good gifts to your children, how much more will your Father in heaven give good gifts to those who ask him!

MATTHEW 7:7-11

When your kids are little, they believe you know everything. That idea brings comfort and security. They think, *Dad is my brilliant, perfect guide through life.*

About the time they get their first cell phone, all that changes. They begin to realize the world is a big and busy place, and Dad can't possibly have all the answers.

You're no longer superhuman, but that's okay. You're something better. A trusted resource. An honest sounding board. A sincere cheerleader. A refuge in any storm.

Older kids may not say it, but they love to hear from Dad. To know you're there. So when you think of them, let 'em know. They are glad you're just a text, phone call, walk down the hallway, or short drive away.

49

BE THERE, DAD.

Children are a gift from the LORD; they are a reward from him. Children born to a young man are like arrows in a warrior's hands. How joyful is the man whose quiver is full of them! He will not be put to shame when he confronts his accusers at the city gates.

PSALM 127:3-5 NLT

Children are a gift, a reward from God. Believe it or not, a certain number of fathers see children as a burden. They are horrified by baby spit on their sport coat. They have no desire to dance with their daughter in the kitchen or at her wedding. The idea of playing catch with their son is not even on their radar. I feel sorry for those men, and I wonder what went wrong.

Maybe they never had an involved father and therefore have no inkling about the joys of fatherhood. Maybe, for some reason, they barely know their children. Maybe those men have been caught up by some worldly distraction.

Gentlemen, step one is *accept the gift*. Step two is to *be there*, starting today. It's not too late.

STOP AND CATCH THE FIREFLIES. LAUGH WITH THEM. CRY WITH THEM. GIVE NOOGIES.

ANSWER THEIR QUESTIONS WITH QUESTIONS. DON'T CURSE THE TRAIN, COUNT THE CARS.

SPY ON YOUR KIDS. BUY A UNICYCLE.

SNUGGLE. RESPECT THEIR MOM.

LAUGH OVER SPILT MILK. QUIT SMOKING.

RESPOND TO ANY CRISIS, "I LOVE YOU. IT'LL BE OKAY. WE'LL GET THROUGH THIS TOGETHER."

HOLD YOUR BABY. TUCK IN. SAY BEDTIME PRAYERS.

RAKE LEAVES TOGETHER. STOP RAKING TO WATCH THE GEESE FLY SOUTH IN "V" FORMATION.

IGNORE THE STICKBALL DENTS ON THE GARAGE DOOR.

WAKE YOUR KID FOR A LUNAR ECLIPSE. MAKE STILTS.

SUDDENLY YOUR 8-YEAR-OLD IS LOOKING YOU IN THE EYE.

QUIT GOLF. OR PATIENTLY TEACH THEM TO PLAY GOLF.

TEACH ROCK/PAPER/SCISSORS. TELL KNOCK-KNOCK JOKES. GIVE HORSEY RIDES.

PLAY H-O-R-S-E.

DON'T LET THEM WIN. THEY'LL BEAT YOU FAIR AND SQUARE SOON ENOUGH.

KISS YOUR WIFE IN THE KITCHEN.

DON'T BE THE JERK IN THE STANDS.

CHAPERONE A SCHOOL DANCE.

The DAD MANIFESTO

52 THINGS FOR FOREVER FATHERS TO NEVER FORGET

EARN THE RIGHT TO SAY WHAT NEEDS TO BE SAID.

CHAT OVER WAFFLES.

STOP AT HISTORICAL MARKERS.

CUDDLE.

SKIP ROCKS. ALWAYS HAVE A CLEAN HANDKERCHIEF.

VOLUNTEER AT THEIR SCHOOL OR YOUTH GROUP.

WRITE "LOVE YOU" ON A STICKY NOTE. APOLOGIZE

KEEP PROMISES. SOMETIMES SAY NO. WHEN YOU MESS UP.

RESCUE THEM AT THE TOP OF ANY SLIPPERY SLOPE.

MAKE TIME FOR THEM. CARRY RECENT PHOTOS

THEY'LL MAKE TIME FOR YOU LATER. ON YOUR SMARTPHONE.

BE AMAZED WHEN THEY BRING YOU A BUG, DANDELION, OR SHINY ROCK.

MAKE YOUR HOME A HANGOUT.

CALL, TEXT, OR REACH OUT TO THEM RIGHT NOW.

BE THERE, DAD. BE AN AWESOME GRANDPA.

TEACH THEM HOW TO LOVE.

TEACH THEM HOW TO BE LOVED.

50

BE AN AWESOME GRANDPA.

*Grandchildren are the crowning glory of the aged;
parents are the pride of their children.*
PROVERBS 17:6 NLT

With your own children, you're too busy being a dad to think about your legacy. But when your kids have kids, it changes everything. You begin to really think about how you will be remembered by future generations.

Briefly, here's how to secure your place in the hearts and minds of your grandkids.

- Be in their life. Be intentional about quality and quantity time.
- Start new traditions. From feeding ducks to monster truck rallies. From story time at the library to season tickets at Wrigley Field.
- Identify a special place you can talk and dream with them. A workshop, garden, home office, porch swing.
- Instead of buying a red Corvette when you turn 60, buy a minivan with seat belts for all your grandkids.
- Tell them how God has worked in your life.

STOP AND CATCH THE FIREFLIES. LAUGH WITH THEM. CRY WITH THEM. GIVE NOOGIES.

ANSWER THEIR QUESTIONS WITH QUESTIONS. DON'T CURSE THE TRAIN, COUNT THE CARS.

SPY ON YOUR KIDS. BUY A UNICYCLE.

SNUGGLE. RESPECT THEIR MOM.

LAUGH OVER SPILT MILK. QUIT SMOKING.

RESPOND TO ANY CRISIS, "I LOVE YOU. IT'LL BE OKAY. WE'LL GET THROUGH THIS TOGETHER."

HOLD YOUR BABY. TUCK IN. SAY BEDTIME PRAYERS. RAKE LEAVES TOGETHER. STOP RAKING TO WATCH THE GEESE FLY SOUTH IN "V" FORMATION.

IGNORE THE STICKBALL DENTS ON THE GARAGE DOOR.

WAKE YOUR KID FOR A LUNAR ECLIPSE. MAKE STILTS. SUDDENLY YOUR 8-YEAR-OLD IS LOOKING YOU IN THE EYE.

QUIT GOLF. OR PATIENTLY TEACH THEM TO PLAY GOLF.

TEACH ROCK/PAPER/SCISSORS. TELL KNOCK-KNOCK JOKES. GIVE HORSEY RIDES.

PLAY H-O-R-S-E. DON'T LET THEM WIN. THEY'LL BEAT YOU FAIR AND SQUARE SOON ENOUGH.

KISS YOUR WIFE IN THE KITCHEN. DON'T BE THE JERK IN THE STANDS. CHAPERONE A SCHOOL DANCE.

EARN THE RIGHT TO SAY WHAT NEEDS TO BE SAID.

CHAT OVER WAFFLES. CUDDLE.

STOP AT HISTORICAL MARKERS.

SKIP ROCKS. ALWAYS HAVE A CLEAN HANDKERCHIEF.

VOLUNTEER AT THEIR SCHOOL OR YOUTH GROUP.

WRITE "LOVE YOU" ON A STICKY NOTE. APOLOGIZE

KEEP PROMISES. SOMETIMES SAY NO. WHEN YOU MESS UP.

RESCUE THEM AT THE TOP OF ANY SLIPPERY SLOPE.

MAKE TIME FOR THEM. THEY'LL MAKE TIME FOR YOU LATER. CARRY RECENT PHOTOS ON YOUR SMARTPHONE.

BE AMAZED WHEN THEY BRING YOU A BUG, DANDELION, OR SHINY ROCK. MAKE YOUR HOME A HANGOUT. CALL, TEXT, OR REACH OUT TO THEM RIGHT NOW.

BE THERE, DAD. BE AN AWESOME GRANDPA.

TEACH THEM HOW TO LOVE.

TEACH THEM HOW TO BE LOVED.

The DAD MANIFESTO 52 THINGS FOR FOREVER FATHERS TO NEVER FORGET

The Dad Manifesto © 2014
Words by Jay Payleitner
AuthorJPayleitner.com
Design by Ron Davis, studiogearbox.com

51

TEACH THEM HOW TO LOVE.

*Everyone who loves has been born of God
and knows God. Whoever does not love does
not know God, because God is love.*

1 JOHN 4:7-8

If you've been paying attention at all, you will have realized that *The Dad Manifesto* is all about loving your kids. From catching fireflies to quitting smoking to rescuing them from serious trouble. Do these things (and more), and you're well on your way to teaching and modeling love to your kids.

But the lesson can't just stop with *acts* of love. Your kids need to know the *source* of love. They need to know that the Creator designed each of us to love, but we can do that only if God has changed our hearts through grace.

Only after you accept God's love can you finally fully love your children. What's more, when you consider how much love you have for your children, you get just a glimpse of how much God loves you.

52

TEACH THEM HOW TO BE LOVED.

God showed his great love for us by sending
Christ to die for us while we were still sinners.

ROMANS 5:8 NLT

It's tragic how many kids grow up feeling unlovable. They spend their entire lives trying to earn love, never realizing they already have the unconditional love of the Creator of the universe.

That's right. God knows everything about you and your children and loves you in spite of all those sins and shortcomings. God's love made you. God's love prepared a place in eternity for you. And God's love put Jesus on the cross to pay the price for the sins of every man, woman, and child who puts their faith and trust in him.

He even has a wonderful plan for you and your family and has given you specific gifts, experiences, and talents to make that plan come true. Helping your kids accept God's love is the entire purpose of *The Dad Manifesto*.

Sharing the Dad Manifesto

Posters, Plaques, Travel Mugs
Be inspired by *The Dad Manifesto* in your office, den, or workshop. Or even as you sip your morning coffee. These 52 ideas for forever fathers have inspired posters, plaques, framable art, and travel mugs available in retail stores across the country and through Slingshot Publishing, the largest Christian poster distributor in North America. www.slingshotpublishing.com.

Downloadable PDF
On Jay's website, jaypayleitner.com, you can download an 8.5 by 11 mini-poster of *The Dad Manifesto* (a printable PDF).

Video and Speaking
At jaypayleitner.com, you also can enjoy short video excerpts from the book featuring the author. And you'll find information on how to bring Jay to your area to speak on parenting, marriage, creativity, and *The Dad Manifesto*.

Gift Giving
Contact the author, the publisher, or Slingshot Publishing for quantity orders of any *Dad Manifesto* resources.